WOMEN AND SOCIAL SECURITY

WOMEN AND SOCIAL SECURITY

PROGRESS TOWARDS EQUALITY OF TREATMENT

Anne-Marie Brocas
Anne-Marie Cailloux
Virginie Oget

International Labour Office Geneva

ISBN 92-2-105559-0 (limp cover)
ISBN 92-2-106518-9 (hard cover)

First published 1990

Published in French under the title:
Les femmes et la sécurité sociale: Les progrès de l'égalité de traitement (ISBN 92-2-205559-4), Genève, 1988.

ILO publications can be obtained through major booksellers or ILO local offices in many countries, or direct from ILO Publications, International Labour Office, CH-1211 Geneva 22, Switzerland. A catalogue or list of new publications will be sent free of charge from the above address.

Printed in Switzerland VAU

PREFACE

This study fills a major gap in the international discussions on equality of opportunity and treatment for women workers. For the past 15 years, since the International Women's Year in 1975, world-wide attention has increasingly been paid to a host of issues that affect the status of women. Equal rights, education, health, employment, and participation in development, to name a few, have been reviewed in numerous forums and have spawned a wealth of literature on efforts to promote equality. Within the ILO, understandably, particular emphasis has been devoted to women and the world of work, ranging from non-discrimination in employment and conditions of work to skill acquisition, and access to employment and income-earning activities in all economic sectors in urban and rural areas. A comprehensive examination of women in social security, however, has not yet taken place in international discussions, despite developments in some national legislation and in certain regional organisations. This study therefore is a timely contribution to the overall debate on equality of treatment.

There are other, more compelling reasons why this study is welcome. First, reviewing the bases of most social security systems forces us to consider the relevance today of several traditional concepts of women and the value of their work inside and outside the home. Women have largely been viewed as dependants, whose earnings, if any, are supplementary to the "bread-winner". Womens' work at home—child rearing and care of the aged, household maintenance, small-scale farming—is generally unrecognised as work *per se* and is not seen as an economic activity vital to the survival of households. Values placed on so-called "female occupations" in the formal sector are reflected by low pay, lack of career mobility and precarious employment conditions. These traditional concepts persist in many countries and reinforce long-standing attitudes about women that are at the root of indirect discrimination. If social security systems are to cater for the vast majority of women in the world, these concepts must be dispassionately scrutinised.

Second, as many social security systems are inextricably related to employment, we are obliged to examine anew the place of women in the labour market, their increasing participation in the labour force and the conditions of work of new employment opportunities—and from this to draw implications on the need for social support services and for sharing family responsibilities between men and women, as well as social protection for, say, unemployment and casual labour.

Third, by reviewing the constraints and difficulties in ensuring social security coverage for women, in different sectors and in various forms of work however broadly defined, we are stimulated to seek ways to improve social security systems in general, for women and men. This surely must be our ultimate aim—equality of treatment *and* treatment for all that meets our aspirations for social justice.

This comprehensive study [1] deals essentially with the issue of women and the world of work. As such it provides a welcome impetus to the ILO's programmes on equality of opportunity and treatment for men and women workers and should prompt concrete steps among the ILO's constituents.

S. C. Cornwell,
Special Adviser,
Women Workers' Questions,
ILO

[1] The ILO gratefully acknowledges the contribution of Joan Berent, who translated this study from the original French.

CONTENTS

INTRODUCTION

Since 1919, the year in which the International Labour Conference adopted the first Convention dealing with maternity protection, a series of international instruments concerning the protection of women's rights have been formulated. In the early years, the emphasis was on the maintenance of employment and on safeguarding the health of women during and after childbirth: later on, these instruments took up the cause of equality of opportunity. Since 1965 there has been a movement in favour of genuinely equal rights for women with family responsibilities. This movement gained momentum in the 1970s, leading to the broader notion of "workers with family responsibilities". At the same time, international institutions came to recognise a new concept regarding equal treatment in the field of social security; that equal treatment can only apply to workers who are in identical employment situations. When these situations differ, various steps must be taken to meet the specific needs of the workers in question.

The reasons for this change in approach to the role and status of women lie in the radical changes which have taken place in attitudes to employment and in family relationships. The economic crisis which has affected the industrialised countries since 1974 has not sent women back into their homes. On the contrary, more and more women now participate in the production process. In 1980, 38.7 per cent of the working population in the OECD countries was female (despite a drop in employment rates for younger women, who are staying longer in full-time education), whereas in 1950 the corresponding percentage was only 31.4. What is more, today's economic climate quite clearly affects both the development and the pattern of female employment. Women now wish to possess their own financial resources just as men do. Although the situation in the developing countries is more difficult to grasp from the data available, it would seem that similar developments are taking place, with more and more women taking up paid employment—although the numbers engaged in agriculture and trading are still high.

Far-reaching changes have also taken place in the industrialised countries as regards the structure, composition and role of the family. Traditional family patterns are giving way to new attitudes and behaviour. There are fewer and fewer large families; birth rates are falling and divorce rates rising. In the developing countries, however, these trends are much less marked.

Equality of treatment for men and women: such has been the driving force behind the progress accomplished over recent years. To what degree has the equality principle found expression in social security policies? To what extent is there still a need for specifically female forms of protection? These are the two broad questions we shall be examining in this study. It covers the period from 1976 to 1985, that of the United Nations Decade for Women. Because of the diversity of situations in which women find themselves and the limits imposed by the amount of information available, the analysis will be mainly concerned with the industrialised countries. Nevertheless, whenever possible, it will be illustrated by significant examples drawn from the developing countries.

PART ONE

A NEW PRINCIPLE IN SOCIAL SECURITY: EQUAL TREATMENT FOR MEN AND WOMEN

It is mainly since 1975 that certain basic questions concerning women's rights in social security have come to the fore and various new goals have been defined. Recognition of the new role played by women in economic, social and cultural development had led to a questioning of the old standards and attitudes, which by then no longer matched the reality. As regards social security, the movement which was getting under way aimed to secure equal rights for the new generations of women wishing to take up paid employment on the same terms as their male counterparts.

Since that time, the principle of equal treatment for men and women in social security has received international approval and has exercised a growing influence on social protection. In many countries it is today embodied in the law of the land. But while the achievements in standard setting should not be underestimated, it is only by close, almost day-to-day examination of the manner in which the equality principle is actually applied that its real impact can be measured.

THE NOTION OF EQUAL TREATMENT: PROGRESS AT INTERNATIONAL LEVEL

1

Equal treatment for men and women has been one of the preoccupations of the major international organisations ever since their foundation. Historically speaking, it was these organisations which led the way. They were joined in their efforts by most of the other intergovernmental institutions, which approached the question with varying degrees of diligence and determination, particularly as regards equality of social protection.

WORLD-WIDE INTERNATIONAL ORGANISATIONS

The first provisions concerning the protection of women appeared towards the end of the nineteenth and the beginning of the twentieth centuries. At its very first session in 1919, the International Labour Conference adopted the Maternity Protection Convention (No. 3), which dealt with the employment of women before and after confinement. Since then, the need to protect the health of women workers at the time of childbirth, to safeguard their employment and to shelter them from material worries has been recognised in the Constitutions of a considerable number of countries, as it was, in general terms, in the 1948 Universal Declaration of Human Rights (article 25, paragraph 2).

Although to begin with the emphasis was on the need to protect women, the International Labour Organisation has invariably associated this concern with that of promoting equality between men and women. The principle of equal wages, without regard to sex, for work of equal value was laid down when the Organisation was first founded, in the general principles governing conditions of work, and was then incorporated into the Preamble to the ILO Constitution. With the adoption in 1944 of the Declaration of Philadelphia defining the aims and purposes of the Organisation, the general principle of equality of opportunity and treatment for men and women was approved internationally for the first time. In that Declaration, the International Labour Conference proclaimed that "all human beings, irrespective of race, creed or sex, have the right to pursue their material well-being and their spiritual development in conditions of freedom and dignity, of economic security and equal opportunity". A first solemn step had been taken towards the progressive confirmation of this principle, at a time when the position of women in society was undergoing a radical change. It is now recognised at the very highest international level that women should no longer merely be the object of special protective measures; they have become complete social beings in their own right.

In international labour standards, the principle of equal treatment for men and women found expression in 1951 in the Equal Remuneration Convention (No. 100), and Recommendation (No. 90), and in 1958 in the Discrimination (Employment and Occupation) Convention (No. 111), and Recommendation (No. 111). Convention No. 111 aims to promote equality in matters of employment and occupation; the definition of these terms is considered broad enough to include social security, and Recommendation No. 111 expressly mentions the social security measures to be provided in connection with employment. It was on the basis of this Convention that the ILO Committee of Experts on the Application of Conventions and Recommendations called for the abolition of certain discriminatory provisions (based on political opinion) concerning social security benefits. However, in view of the complexity of the problems involved, the Committee refrained from assessing the impact on equal treatment of men and women in social security of the very general provisions contained in Convention No. 111.

It was no doubt natural that attention should first be concentrated on the question of access to, and the exercise of, employment since discrimination in that field was particularly striking and the need for action particularly urgent. The order in which problems arise during the course of working life may also have been a reason for broaching the question of unequal treatment in employment before that of any inequalities that might exist in social security.

Even though the latter concern has not yet resulted in the drafting of a binding international instrument dealing expressly with equal treatment for men and women in social security, it is being voiced more and more clearly at international level, especially since 1975, a year which constitutes a turning-point in the history of contemporary thinking on the status of women. The movement launched by the United Nations in favour of women's participation in economic and social development has encouraged the adoption of new measures designed to enhance the position of women and to give them a more important part to play in social progress in all its aspects.

In 1975 the World Conference of the International Women's Year was held under United Nations auspices in Mexico City. The Conference adopted a Declaration on the equality of women and their contribution to development and peace, as well as a World Plan of Action to guide the implementation of the objectives of the International Women's Year for the period 1976-85, which was proclaimed the United Nations Decade for Women.[1]

The Plan of Action refers to a number of instruments—adopted, inter alia, by the United Nations and the ILO—in which the international community asks that women should be entitled, on the same terms as men, to participate fully in the development process and that all human beings should, without distinction, enjoy the fruits of economic and social progress. The Plan itself defines equality between men and women as equality of rights, opportunities and responsibilities. Equality, which should be embodied in law, should ensure equal opportunities in education and training, as well as in conditions of employment, including remuneration and social security. Regarding employment, the Plan calls for an end to discrimination against women in social security schemes: these should provide women workers with protection equal in all respects to that of men.

Also in 1975 the International Labour Conference adopted a Declaration on Equality of Opportunity and Treatment for Women Workers, together with a resolution concerning equal status and equal opportunity for women and men in occupation and employment and a resolution concerning a Plan of Action with a view to promoting equality of opportunity and treatment for women workers.[2] These texts indicate the broad principles to be followed and define the steps to be taken to implement and to ensure genuine equality. As regards social protection, they forbid any form of discrimination against women and require the elimination of any differences in treatment that may exist:

> There shall be no discrimination against women in respect of social security and provisions concerning retirement and pensions, and differences in the treatment of men and women under such schemes shall be reviewed and revised (Declaration, article 11).
>
> Measures should be taken to eliminate all discriminatory treatment in social security schemes, in particular as concerns the payment of benefits, and to review the position of heads of families and single persons with regard to entitlement to social security benefits (resolution concerning a Plan of Action, para. 5).

The ILO Medium-Term Plan for the period 1976-81 repeated the recommendations set out in these texts and listed among its priorities the elimination of all discriminatory treatment of women in social security.

The World Conference of the United Nations Decade for Women, held in Copenhagen in 1980, was called upon to evaluate the progress made since the Mexico Conference, five years earlier, and to draw up a Programme of Action for the second half of the Decade, with special emphasis on employment, health and training.[3] The Conference found that, although progress

[1] United Nations: *Report of the World Conference of the International Women's Year,* Mexico City, 19 June-2 July 1975 (New York, 1976).

[2] *Official Bulletin* (Geneva, ILO), Vol. LVIII, 1975, Series A, No. 1.

[3] United Nations: *Report of the World Conference of the United Nations Decade for Women: Equality, Development and Peace,* Copenhagen, 14-30 July 1980 (New York, 1980).

had been achieved and national planners had become more sensitive to women's needs and problems, the progress was insufficient to bring about adequate improvements in the status of women. The Programme of Action reaffirmed the joint responsibility of men and women for the welfare of the family in general, and for the care of their children in particular. It urged governments to accord high priority to accelerating full and equal participation of women in development by associating them more closely in decision-making at all levels and in all sectors. As regards employment, appropriate steps should be taken to extend education and training for women, increase their opportunities for employment, improve their conditions of work and ensure equal treatment. The discussions at the Conference and the texts adopted all appear to be inspired by the same desire: to put an end to any remaining discrimination against women through concerted action at all levels.

Over 70 States took advantage of the Copenhagen Conference to accede to the Convention on the Elimination of all Forms of Discrimination against Women, adopted a short while earlier at the end of 1979, by the United Nations General Assembly.[4] This international instrument, the most comprehensive ever drawn up and adopted by the United Nations on the subject, aims to eliminate—

> any distinction, exclusion or restriction made on the basis of sex which has the effect or purpose of impairing or nullifying the recognition, enjoyment or exercise by women, irrespective of their marital status, on a basis of equality of men and women, of human rights and fundamental freedoms in the political, economic, social, cultural, civil or any other field (Article 1).

Concerning employment, the Convention calls for equality of rights for men and women, in particular as regards the right to social security, especially in cases of retirement, unemployment, sickness, invalidity and old age, or any other incapacity to work (Article 11).

The ILO Medium-Term Plan for the period 1982-87 attached major importance to the problems of economically active women. Three main lines of action were proposed: to bring about a better understanding of the nature and degree of discrimination against women in employment and of its harmful consequences in economic and social development; to maximise equality of treatment between the sexes; and to facilitate the entry of women into working life. Regarding the setting of standards, the Plan sets out three ways of promoting equality of treatment: stricter application of existing laws; the possibility of drawing up new international standards of a general character; the adoption or revision of standards on special subjects. Consideration was also to be given, towards the end of the period, to the study of standards concerning women's social security rights.

---

[4] idem: *Resolutions and Decisions adopted by the General Assembly during its Thirty-Fourth Session,* 18 September 1979-7 January 1980, General Assembly, Official Records, 34th Session, Supplement No. 46 (A/34/46) (New York, 1980), pp. 193-198.

In 1985, at the close of the United Nations Decade for Women, a World Conference was convened in Nairobi to appraise the achievements and to work out forward-looking strategies for the advancement of women up to the year 2000. With reference to equality, the Conference recalled that one of the Decade's objectives had been to achieve full observance of equal rights for women and the elimination of *de jure* and *de facto* discrimination against them. It invited governments to ensure, for both men and women, equality before the law, equality of educational opportunities, training and health services, and equality of employment, including remuneration and social security.[5]

In that same year the 71st Session of the International Labour Conference adopted a resolution on equal opportunities and equal treatment for men and women in employment in which it evaluated the progress achieved since the adoption of the Plan of Action ten years earlier and indicated some of the steps still to be taken.[6] As regards social security, the Conference requested that, in cases where women receive unequal social security benefits, specific measures should be taken to remedy the situation. Such measures might include: the provision of adequate resources with a view to providing social security coverage appropriate to the needs of women workers; the development of social security systems in such a way as to ensure equal treatment for men and women by prohibiting direct or indirect discrimination regardless of marital or family status; the gradual extension of social security coverage to workers not covered or only partly covered.

It is clear, then, that as regards women's place in the modern world and the exercise of their social rights, the notion of equality of treatment for men and women progressed considerably at the highest international level during the period 1975-85, and that this has contributed greatly to the advancement of the equal rights principle in the domain of social security.

This progress has not, however, led to the establishment of formal ILO standards or of a binding international instrument dealing specifically with equal treatment of men and women in social security. The delay is no doubt regrettable, in that it deprives individual countries of a framework of standards and internationally applicable rules setting out precise priorities and objectives, the need for which, after so many years of discussion and activity regarding the social status of women, can no longer be denied. There are, however, grounds for hope that within the next few years the matter will be placed on the agenda of the International Labour Conference and that such an instrument will be adopted.

---

[5] idem: *Report of the World Conference to Review and Appraise the Achievements of the United Nations Decade for Women: Equality, Development and Peace,* Nairobi, 15-26 July 1985 (New York, 1986).

[6] *Official Bulletin* (Geneva, ILO), Vol. LXVIII, 1985, Series A, No. 2.

REGIONAL ORGANISATIONS

Organisation for Economic Co-operation and Development

In 1980 the OECD held a High-Level Conference in Paris on the subject of female employment. It adopted a communiqué and published a Declaration on the policies to be followed.[7]

The communiqué stressed that women and men, as equal members of society, should have equal opportunities for paid employment, independently of the rate of economic growth and conditions in the labour market; the right to support oneself and to contribute to the economic well-being of one's family was as important for women as for men.

The Declaration listed the aims to be given priority consideration in the formation of member States' policies in the following fields: employment, unemployment, remuneration, working hours, social security, training, re-entry into the labour market, protection of women in law, maternity protection, and others. In order to eliminate segregation in matters of employment, the Conference recommended that all direct discrimination should be prohibited by law, that positive action should be taken to reduce indirect discrimination in recruitment, training and promotion and that efforts should be made to combat persistent social biases and negative institutional practices.

The European Communities

The action undertaken by the European Communities to secure recognition of the principle that men and women should be treated equally in social security has led not only to declarations of principles, but also to the adoption of standards which are binding on the member States. Although, as will be seen, their work of standardisation cannot be considered as complete, the Communities are at this time the bodies which have drawn up the tightest legal framework at supranational level. Repeating almost word for word the terms of Convention No. 100 (1951), Article 119 of the Treaty of Rome introduces into the European Communities' legal system the principle of equal remuneration for men and women for work of equal value. This is the only express indication of a desire to improve the status of women in the founding texts of the Communities.

Recognition of the equal pay principle constituted the starting-point from which Community action to achieve equality of opportunity and treatment between men and women began. As regards social security, the Communities chose to draw up specific instruments for all schemes: legal and statutory schemes, but also occupational schemes.

---

[7] OECD, High-level Conference on the Employment of Women, Paris, 16-17 April 1980, press release, PRESS/A(80)26.

The decisive text was the Directive issued by the Council of the European Communities on 19 December 1978 regarding the progressive implementation of the principle of equal treatment for men and women in matters of social security. This was followed by the Directive submitted to the Council on 5 May 1983, which extended application of this principle to occupational schemes (the Directive was adopted on 24 July 1986), and by a proposal for a Directive put before the Council on 15 March 1984 concerning application of the equal treatment principle to self-employed men and women, including those engaged in agriculture, and to the protection of maternity. Extension of the principle to benefits not covered by the 1978 Directive is under study. From 1982 to 1985 the European Communities carried out their first programme of action to achieve equality of opportunity and this effort is being pursued in the second programme of action, which covers the years 1986-90.

Under the terms of the Directive of 19 December 1978 (79/7/EEC),[8] which covered statutory schemes providing protection against the risks of sickness, invalidity, old age, accidents at work, occupational diseases and unemployment, and social assistance in so far as it is intended to supplement or replace the foregoing, member States were required, within a period of six years, to abolish all legislative, statutory or administrative provisions contrary to the principle of equal treatment. Particular attention was to be paid to the scope and conditions of access to each scheme, the obligation to contribute, the calculation of contributions and benefits, and the conditions governing the duration and retention of entitlement to benefits. Provisions relating to maternity protection were not considered to be discriminatory.

The Directive applies to the whole working population, including the self-employed. In some respects its scope is limited. It does not refer to provisions concerning survivors' benefits or family benefits. Most important of all, the Directive is not binding on member States, which makes it possible for them to maintain differences in treatment in certain sensitive areas: the determination of retirement age; the advantages granted to persons who have brought up children (old-age insurance); the acquisition of benefit entitlements following periods of interruption of employment spent bringing up children; the granting of derived entitlements to wives (old age, invalidity); and long-term increments to benefits for dependent spouses (invalidity, old age, work accidents and occupational diseases). It is clear that these limitations are serious, in that they concern sensitive issues where the greatest inequalities are to be found. Member States were asked to examine them periodically, in the light of social developments, to ascertain whether they should be maintained.

---

[8] *Official Journal of the European Communities* (Luxembourg), No. L6, 10 Jan. 1979, pp. 24-25.

The Council Directive of 24 July 1986 (86/378/EEC)[9] concerned the implementation of the principle of equal treatment for men and women in occupational social security schemes, whether membership of such schemes is compulsory or optional. Situated somewhere between statutory schemes and private insurance, occupational schemes include those instituted under collective agreements at the level of the enterprise, area of economic activity or occupational sector or group, schemes set up by employers—if necessary through an insurance company—and schemes applying to certain unpaid occupations.

As regards the branches covered, the Directive concerns the same schemes (this time referring to occupations) as the preceding one (it also covers, for paid employees, schemes providing other benefits, survivors' benefits and family allowances in particular, if such benefits are accorded by reason of the employment). The individual scope of coverage is the same as in the earlier Directive, but the text is more restrictive. It declares contrary to the principle of equal treatment any suspension of the retention or acquisition of rights during periods of maternity leave or leave for family reasons. As regards determination of the retirement age for the purposes of granting old-age or retirement pensions, it allows member States to defer only temporarily the application of the principle. Lastly, it allows them three years in which to introduce the necessary changes.

On 15 March 1984 the Commission of the European Communities submitted to the Council a proposal for a Directive on the application of the principle of equal treatment for men and women engaged in an activity, including agriculture, in a self-employed capacity, and on maternity protection for self-employed women. The Directive (86/613/EEC) was adopted on 11 December 1986.[10]

The text covers self-employed persons, that is to say, all persons pursuing a gainful activity on their own account, including farmers and members of the liberal professions and—and this is the most important aspect—their spouses when they participate "to a significant extent" in the activities of the self-employed worker and perform the same or ancillary tasks without a partnership agreement or contract of employment. It asks member States to take all the measures necessary to ensure that spouses are able to build up an independent entitlement as regards social security, including the right to maternity benefits, and that women self-employed workers and the spouses of self-employed workers should, during interruptions in their occupational activity due to pregnancy or maternity, be able to call on relief services or be entitled to appropriate benefits under a social security scheme, or any other public system of social protection. All persons who consider themselves affected by failure to apply the principle of equal treatment in self-

[9] ibid., No. L225, 12 Aug. 1986, pp. 40-42.

[10] ibid., No. C113, 27 Apr. 1984, pp. 4-6.

employed occupations should be able to pursue their claims by judicial process after possible recourse to other competent authorities.

For the very first time, the proposed Directive deals with persons whose work is not recognised as an occupational activity and who enjoy neither the status of partner (unpaid) nor that of the spouse's employee. It undoubtedly represents progress in relation to the previous Directives, which covered only persons exercising an activity sanctioned by the payment of wages and which totally excluded participating spouses.

At the same time, the Commission of the European Communities had a study made of the implementation of the equal treatment principle in benefits not covered by the 1978 Directive and in matters, as described above, that might be excluded from its purview. The report on the subject lists instances of discrimination and suggests solutions to *de facto* inequalities, which might be dealt with in a second directive concerning statutory social security schemes.[11]

The drafting of proposed Directives for 1983 and 1984 was part of the general Action Programme to promote equal opportunities, adopted by the European Communities for the period 1982-85.[12] This Programme was drawn up during a period of economic and social difficulties when many women were in precarious forms of employment and were affected by cuts in public expenditure on social infrastructures. It aimed to achieve equality of opportunity and treatment by strengthening the rights of the individual woman and, in practice, by means of a series of positive actions. To help in the task, the Commission set up an Advisory Committee on Equal Opportunities for Men and Women. The Action Programme emphasised the need to increase awareness of the positive aspects of changes in attitudes to the sharing of occupational, family and social responsibilities and, as far as social security is concerned, set guide-lines for harmonisation of country standards. It also invited member States to take measures to extend the principle of equal treatment to schemes which were not covered by the 1978 Directive.

For the period 1986-90 the European Communities have adopted a second Action Programme, aimed at intensifying and developing the action already undertaken, with a view to achieving genuine equality so that women can approach today's social, technological and occupational change on an equal footing with men.[13]

---

[11] *La mise en œuvre de l'égalité de traitement entre hommes et femmes en matière de sécurité sociale en ce qui concerne les prestations non soumises à la Directive 79/7/EEC du 19 décembre 1978: inventaire et propositions,* Definitive synthesis report by Ms. C. Même, doc. V/1261/84-FR (Brussels, Commission of the European Communities, July 1984).

[12] Commission of the European Communities: *Equal opportunities. Action Programme 1982-1985,* Supplement No. 9 to *Women of Europe,* doc. 41/X/82-EN (Brussels, 1982).

[13] idem: *Equal Opportunities. Second Action Programme 1986-1990,* Supplement No. 23 to *Women of Europe,* doc. X/77/86-EN (Brussels, 1986).

As regards social protection, the programme sets out three broad guidelines for action: to reform social security budgets so that they do not have a discriminatory effect in relation to women; to promote the gradual acquisition by women of individual rights so as to eliminate indirect discrimination; to reinforce provisions for the protection of pregnancy and maternity so as to provide adequate protection and eliminate discriminatory effects on recruitment and career advancement. The Commission is to pursue its work on the drafting of a new legal instrument intended, in particular, to supplement the existing provisions in the areas not covered by the 1978 Directive.

THE PRINCIPLE OF EQUAL TREATMENT: IMPLEMENTATION AT NATIONAL LEVEL

2

The extensive normative action undertaken at international level has inevitably influenced national legal practices, as political leaders and economic and social authorities become increasingly aware of the need for unequivocal recognition of the position and presence of women in all walks of economic and social life. The principle that men and women should receive equal treatment has begun to take hold in national social security legislation, although progress has not been nearly as rapid as it has been internationally or, at country level, in the sphere of labour law.

In order to gain a clearer understanding of the issues involved, some consideration must be given to certain particularities of the laws concerning social protection. Special attention will need to be paid to the conditions governing women's access to the labour market, which go a long way towards explaining the difficulty of putting the equal treatment principle into effect. Only then can an attempt be made to provide a functional definition of the principle as it affects social security and to state the goals to be pursued when introducing new measures at national level.

EQUAL TREATMENT: RECOGNITION OF THE PRINCIPLE

Chapter 1 traced the progress of the concept of equal treatment internationally. This international progress has been followed up, at country level, by the adoption of new legal standards, by the formulation of plans of action in favour of women and by the setting up of diverse bodies to discuss the problems and initiate changes.

The general principle

The principle that men and women should be equal in all spheres—political, economic, social and cultural—is in many countries written into the basic laws of the land. To mention only a few of the texts adopted during the period covered by this study, it is embodied in Algeria's 1976 Constitution, in Portugal's Constitution of the same year, in the new paragraph inserted in the Swiss Constitution in 1981, in the 1977 Constitution (basic law) of the USSR, and in Viet Nam's Constitution of 1981.

As far as social legislation is concerned, the principle of equal treatment for men and women is referred to—again to mention only a few of the texts adopted since 1975—in Australia in Law No. 9027 of 24 May 1977, in the German Democratic Republic in the Labour Code adopted on 16 June 1977, in Luxembourg in the law of 8 December 1981, in the Netherlands in the law of 1 March 1981, and in Norway in Law No. 45 passed on 9 June 1978.

The legislative provisions have been reinforced in a number of countries during the period under study by general policy declarations or plans of action designed to promote equality of treatment.

Thus, in October 1976 the Government of Pakistan published a Declaration of Women's Rights setting out the rights of the female population in all areas of political, legal, economic and social life and, in its Preamble, forbidding any form of discrimination against women.

In February 1977 the Japanese Government approved a ten-year plan of action intended to provide a social climate in which women would be able to enjoy the same rights as men, in application of the United Nations World Plan of Action.

In March 1982 Senegal's National Assembly ratified a national plan of action concerning women, which specifies the objectives to be pursued in the various economic sectors with regard to their training, health, nutrition and the creation of jobs.

Such resolutions, of which the foregoing are only three examples, have been followed up in several countries by practical measures setting up the administrative machinery needed to implement the proposed programmes, with the help of government bodies and other relevant institutions.

In putting these plans of action into effect, the impetus often comes from parliamentary commissions and other committees dealing with matters of concern to women which have been set up in almost all parts of the world—in Austria, Belgium, France, the Federal Republic of Germany, Norway, Portugal and the USSR, as well as in Côte d'Ivoire, Papua New Guinea and Uruguay. New study and action groups have been created to examine the situation and initiate the social and economic reforms needed to ensure equality between the sexes. Between 1975 and 1985 many countries set up stable administrative structures—ministerial departments or bureaux—to deal with women's issues. These include such dissimilar countries as, for instance, Canada, Cuba, France, Jamaica, Japan, Norway and Venezuela.

Employment and social protection

The adoption of legal standards, the drafting of plans of action, the setting up of new study groups and advisory bodies—all these measures bear witness to the growing importance attached to the status of women. They are evidence of new social attitudes, but tend to be very general in their scope, covering all political, economic, social and cultural domains.

In the social sector as such, States—following the example of the international bodies—have devoted most of their attention to proclaiming and guaranteeing equal treatment for men and women in employment, the object being to ensure that women enjoy the same opportunities as men in obtaining access to training and employment and in the choice of occupation.

Discriminatory practices in employment on the grounds of sex are dealt with in detail in many national legislations: they are to be "outlawed"; national courts must declare them invalid, and this ruling usually goes together with a fine.

No such far-reaching provisions exist with regard to social protection: there are several explanations for this.

The first no doubt stems from the nature of the two branches of legislation involved. In most countries labour law governs mainly the relations between private individuals, covering an infinite variety of particular situations. Law-makers must legislate in such a way as to guarantee respect for the general principle of equality of treatment. The object of social security legislation, on the other hand, is to maintain the living standards of protected persons in the event of a whole series of contingencies. Responsibility for, and management of, the system lie with States or with collective welfare institutions. Their action is addressed to groups of individuals who find themselves in objectively defined situations.

The measures adopted invariably involve considerable financial outlay. Such financial considerations no doubt explain why progress in defining the principle of equal treatment in social security and embodying it in the law has been slower than in the employment sector and why there has been some delay in establishing the prime responsibility of governments in matters of social security—since these appear to be less pressing.

The other major explanation must be sought in the particular conditions governing women's access to the labour market, which make it difficult to interpret the equal treatment principle in terms of social security standards.

THE SPECIFIC NATURE OF FEMALE EMPLOYMENT

Since the end of the Second World War most parts of the world have seen a considerable increase in the number of women taking an active part in economic life. This development, which has often been described and analysed, can be illustrated by the figures for the OECD countries, where the percentage of women gainfully employed rose from 31.4 in 1950 to 38.7 in 1980.[1]

But although the activity rates for women have risen, the structure of female employment has undergone little change. Women workers continue to be concentrated in a fairly small number of occupations, which often require few skills and are poorly paid. This situation has been aggravated by the economic recession.

Most of the increase in female employment has occurred in the service sector, which has expanded greatly over the past 20 years. The influx of women workers has been especially marked in the public and parastatal sectors, where the criteria for recruitment and the conditions of work are less disadvantageous to them than in other fields. The considerable sums allotted to health services, social protection and education have led to the creation of a large number of jobs, many of which have been taken up by women. The widespread development of employment connected with the operation of social transfers has everywhere been dominated by women.

The growth of female employment, particularly in services and the public sector, can also be explained by a marked demand for part-time work and, more generally speaking, for "flexible" working schedules. These sectors lend themselves especially well to such arrangements, in that the volume of work may fluctuate according to the hour or the day, for example, or because of the new operating methods and forms of work organisation made possible by modern data-processing methods and telematics, such as telework (home-based work linked to a computer). The response to this demand for workers in part-time, temporary or casual jobs and home work—forms of work which offer many advantages to employers—has been greater among women than among men.

Women's working lives are marked, more often than those of men, by alternating periods of economic activity and inactivity, although of late there has been a trend towards greater stability. Women, particularly younger women, now remain in work more often and remain longer. Marriage is no longer an obstacle to the exercise of an occupation. In fact, the employment rates for married women have risen more rapidly than those for women in general (it is true, however, that they often occupy part-time posts). A similar trend has been observed among women with children. The number of mothers in jobs has increased considerably, although the need to care for small children still results in some periods of withdrawal from the labour force. The labour force participation rate for women with children under the age of 7, whether married or not, more than doubled in the OECD countries between the early 1960s and the early 1980s.[2] To a large

---

[1] L. Paukert: *Employment and unemployment of women in OECD countries* (Paris, OECD, 1984).

[2] ibid.

extent, this has been made possible by the development of collective child-care facilities.

The rapid growth of female participation in economic activity, despite the tightness of the labour market, is the direct and irreversible consequence of the social and economic changes that have taken place over the past few decades. In spite of the recession, women have not relinquished their right to work, as can be seen from the large numbers who register as unemployed. This being said, however, the vagaries of the economic climate, advances in technology and changing patterns of employment have greatly influenced the opportunities for, and conditions of female access to, paid work, making women even more vulnerable as far as employment is concerned.

To the extent that they halt the expansion of public and parastatal sectors, the social services in particular, national policies aimed at cutting back government expenditure particularly affect women workers, who are especially numerous in these fields. Technical innovations and the spread of automation in public and other services call for new skills and are thus a threat to many posts that are mainly occupied by women. Current developments tend to channel women, especially the youngest among them, into specific patterns of activity which give rise to discriminatory situations. Part-time work, casual work and home work all offer little prospect of promotion; women employed on such work often suffer from frequent periods of unemployment and, generally speaking, remain outside the mainstream of the labour market.

This study, as was pointed out in the Introduction, deals mainly with industrialised countries. It is not without interest, however, to mention here some of the characteristic features of female employment in developing countries.

In rural areas, where most of the population lives, women are engaged in various agricultural activities, which more often than not lie outside the scope of any social protection. In addition, there is such work as the processing and packaging of agricultural produce, weaving and the sale of goods produced, all of which are extensions of the tasks women carry out in their homes.

In the developing countries, as almost everywhere, traditional activities are in decline and paid employment is on the increase, with a concomitant flow of rural populations to the towns. It is as members of the urban labour force that women are becoming—or ought to become—increasingly integrated into the employment milieu, a trend which is helped along by the policies for advancement and education introduced in their favour. Job opportunities in the modern sector are, however, still very limited. Many women are occupied in the informal sector, with no guarantee of stable employment, or in activities which escape the attention of regulatory bodies, either because the scale is so small and they have no fixed structures, or because they are mobile, seasonal or even illegal. In some of the larger cities a considerable share of the working population is engaged in such "unstructured" activities, and many of these workers are women.

As will be shown throughout this study, the specific nature of female employment has an immediate direct impact on the social protection accorded to women. The sectors of activity in which they are employed, their job structures and the terms of their employment all place women in situations which hamper the implementation of equal treatment in social security. This fact must lead us to qualify somewhat the objectives to be assigned to equal treatment policies in this field.

WHAT IS MEANT BY EQUAL TREATMENT IN SOCIAL SECURITY?

The first definition which springs to mind might be expressed as follows: equal social rights in equal situations. The difficulty of assessing "equality" in the situations of men and women is immediately apparent. Another question which arises is whether it is legitimate to establish general reference standards for men against which the position of women and the treatment they are to receive should be measured.

In fact, little uniformity or equality of situations exists among men themselves. The social security entitlements available to them often vary widely according to socio-occupational category or the type of social security scheme to which they belong. There is little practical interest, as far as the subject under study is concerned, in considering either the male population as a whole or the female population as a whole.

On the other hand, much is to be learned from comparing the protection accorded to men and that accorded to women within each branch of activity and within each social security scheme; any discrimination discovered will then be of real significance.

These general considerations have led us to circumscribe our study, limiting it to the only situation for which valid comparisons are possible: that of persons exercising an occupational activity.

This deliberate decision to restrict the scope of the study means leaving aside other situations characteristic of women's status, including the position of those who remain at home. Furthermore, comparisons can only be made between social security schemes and their benefits when such comparisons make sense, which of course excludes maternity protection. These aspects of the subject will be taken up in Part Two of the study, which examines some of the specific areas in which, in the present state of affairs, women's needs for protection are still not fully satisfied.

The question we shall be trying to answer in Part One is, therefore, as follows: Do men and women who are in the same employment situation enjoy equal rights within the social security scheme applying to them? This will lead us to consider to what extent social security policies have sought, if not to offset, at least not to aggravate the discrimination women encounter at work.

Equal treatment will be considered to exist when all women engaged in a particular activity are entitled, on the same terms as men, to protection against all the social risks covered by the relevant scheme—whatever the form of activity or the economic sector in which they are employed—and when in social security schemes the same rules apply to both men and women whenever they find themselves in identical situations with regard to their employment (and, incidentally, with regard to the contributions they have paid).

It is from this viewpoint that the following chapter assesses the progress made in securing equality of treatment in social security legislation over the period under study.

PROGRESS TOWARDS EQUAL TREATMENT IN SOCIAL SECURITY LEGISLATION 3

Despite the unfavourable economic climate, social coverage of women improved during the period 1975-85, with many States also endeavouring to eliminate some of the discriminatory rules in their social security schemes.

The prime condition for achieving equality of treatment, as defined earlier, is the very existence of social protection for working men and women. The efforts made by States to ensure such protection represent major progress. Such efforts take on an extra dimension when they are directed to those sectors in which women workers are particularly numerous or where they are actually in the majority. Any improvement affecting the branches of activity which employ a large proportion of women is a step towards equality and helps to ensure that all workers in similar employment situations enjoy the same entitlement to social protection, whatever their sex.

In the following pages we shall draw special attention to measures which bring improved social protection to large numbers of women. Various examples will be provided, although the list is by no means exhaustive.

PROGRESS IN SOCIAL PROTECTION

The institution of protection

The prerequisite for equality of treatment is, as we have already said, the very fact that social protection exists. Several countries have introduced such protection during the period under consideration.

Among the countries which have instituted their first basic social security programmes, Seychelles has opted for what is essentially a universal system. The social security scheme set up between 1975 and 1980 covers, for all the contingencies listed, all persons residing in the country who have an income (from employment or other sources). Contributions are paid by each individual in proportion to total income.

Other countries have introduced schemes which cover all persons in paid employment. Inasmuch as it is through paid employment that women become integrated into the labour force, both in developed countries and—increasingly—in developing countries, such programmes are of particular interest to women workers. During the period covered by the study, several developing countries have instituted comprehensive social security systems for employed persons: the Sudan in 1974, Kuwait in 1976, Jordan in 1978, Belize in 1981 and Grenada in 1983. Other countries have broadened already existing schemes covering persons in paid employment, for example Pakistan, which instituted old-age and invalidity insurance in 1976, and Senegal, which in 1975 introduced sickness insurance.

Extension of coverage

Quite a number of countries have extended the coverage offered by their social security systems during the period in question. Such measures are of particular importance to women when they are directed either at the economic sectors that employ a high proportion of women workers or at forms of activity that are almost exclusively female.

Agriculture

In view of the considerable numbers of women engaged in agricultural tasks, special mention should be made of the steps taken to extend social security coverage to the agricultural sector in developing countries and to improve such coverage in industrialised countries. In many cases, the measures adopted cover both persons working for wages and the self-employed.

In Tunisia, for instance, Law No. 81-6 of 12 February 1981 introduced a social security scheme for wage-earning agricultural workers and those engaged in co-operative undertakings. In the following year, this scheme was extended to cover small farmers and the self-employed. In Turkey all agricultural workers, wage earners and self-employed, have been protected by compulsory insurance since 1 January 1984.

Between 1975 and 1983 Bulgaria, Czechoslovakia, Hungary, Poland and Romania gradually extended and improved social security coverage both for workers in agricultural co-operatives and for individual farmers.

In Finland the Law of 23 December 1981 instituted insurance against occupational risks for self-employed agricultural workers and their families. In Greece old-age protection was in 1982 extended to women working in agriculture.

Self-employment

Considerable progress has also been made in improving social security protection for self-employed workers in sectors other than agriculture.

This is the case in Gabon where, since 1983, the self-employed have benefited from a system of social guarantees, and in Tunisia, where social security coverage was extended to self-employed workers in 1982.

In 1975 Portugal introduced its first scheme for the self-employed; in 1981 it brought in a new scheme and two years later instituted protection for the self-employed against the risks of maternity and sickness (cash benefits). In Sweden the legislation governing occupational accidents and diseases was extended to cover the self-employed in 1977, and in 1980 Denmark broadened its laws to provide unemployment benefits for self-employed workers.

Participation in spouse's activity

In many family businesses the help of the spouse (usually the wife) is indispensable, though the income from the business is not always sufficient to pay him or her a proper wage, despite the fact that he or she is actually a partner in the operation. A number of initiatives have been taken at national level which are evidence of a desire to secure recognition of the spouse's contribution to the family enterprise when no company has been formed.

Since 1974 Luxembourg has offered the wives of artisans, tradespeople and small-scale entrepreneurs the option of taking out voluntary old-age insurance, and has made it compulsory for self-employed farmers' wives to join the farm pension scheme as registered assistants. Protection provided under the Canada Pension Plan and the Quebec Pension Plan was in 1981 extended to spouses working in family businesses. Contributions are levied on the spouse's earnings, which are deducted from the owner's taxable income. In France Law No. 82-596 of 10 July 1982 regarding the spouses of artisans and tradespeople who work in the family business stipulates that those concerned, men or women, may exercise their activity as assistants, as wage-earning spouses or as partners, with different civil, commercial, fiscal and social rights and obligations according to their status. The main consequence of this choice of status is that, for social security purposes, the person in question becomes a member either of a wage earners' scheme or of a scheme for those who are not in paid employment.

In Hungary, the decision to broaden coverage in the old-age and invalidity branches in 1982, in the occupational accident branch in 1981-83 and in the sickness branch in 1983 has brought many advantages to the spouses of operators of "small economic units" and "industrial technical groups", as well as to those of individual farmers who contribute on a regular basis to the work of enterprises that have concluded contracts with co-operative undertakings. New arrangements came into force in Poland in 1983, guaranteeing fuller protection to members of the families of self-employed farmers. Children and other family members over the age of 16 who work on the farm are entitled not only to employment injury benefits, but also to old-age and invalidity pensions; the condition that the farm must be handed over to a successor or to the State does not apply—as it would to the farmer himself. Two separate old-age pensions are paid, one to the farmer and one to the spouse, whereas under the previous legislation the pension was divided into two equal parts.

Special forms of paid work

It has already been pointed out that, as part of the process of bringing women into paid employment, certain "modified" forms of activity are being expanded—part-time, temporary and casual work, and home occupations: in fact, these are becoming the normal patterns of activity for many women.

The rapid expansion of such atypical forms of employment has led a number of countries to adopt special regulations to cover them. Since they require adjustment of the labour laws, logically they should also lead to the adjustment of social security provisions. The fact is that whereas, apart from a few isolated cases, the workers occupying such jobs are not formally excluded from social security schemes, the qualifying conditions for entitlement—minimum duration of work in any one month or year, or minimum amount of earnings—are such that they tend to prevent them from enjoying the normal social security benefits. This fact has been much debated in a number of countries.

In Canada, for instance, where part-time work has increased steadily over the past 30 years and where almost three-quarters of part-time jobs are held by women, the Government asked the Canadian Advisory Council on the Status of Women to report on the situation, which it did in 1983. The report showed that part-time workers enjoyed little if any protection in law; the authors felt that the matter had taken on immense importance and should be among the main priorities of the legislators.[1] In March 1974 Japan's Ministry of Labour decided, in view of the growing importance of part-time employment, to draw up a series of directives which would lead to stricter control of this form of work and would ensure protection for part-time workers.[2] In Peru, where almost half of all workers are, in one way or another, casual labourers, a technical meeting held in December 1983 stressed their extremely precarious situation and the need for them to be better protected.[3]

---

[1] *Canadian Industrial Relations and Personnel Developments* (Ottawa), 24 June 1983.

[2] *Asahi Evening News* (Tokyo), 9 Mar. 1984.

[3] Inter-American Centre for Labour Administration – Friedrich-Ebert Stiftung: *Documents de travail de la Réunion technique sur les conséquences de la crise économique pour les travailleurs occasionnels au Pérou, 2–4 décembre 1983.*

During the period 1975-85 similar concerns led a number of countries to introduce social security provisions applying expressly to atypical patterns of work, or at least to some of them. The following cases, which are given by way of example only, help to illustrate the changes taking place.

In 1976 Luxembourg extended unemployment benefits to homeworkers and domestic servants. In Portugal domestic servants have received family allowances since 1978. The compulsory insurance scheme against occupational accidents introduced in Guinea-Bissau in 1980 covers all workers, including part-time workers and domestic employees. In Costa Rica, where Law No. 6727 of 9 March 1982 makes it compulsory for all employers to insure their employees against occupational risks, casual workers, homeworkers and domestic servants are now covered.

In the United Kingdom part-time workers have, since February 1977, enjoyed the same social protection as full-time employees, on condition that they work a minimum number of hours (16 hours a week for the same employer or eight hours a week for the same employer for at least five years). Belgium has introduced a more flexible system and has made adjustments designed to provide better protection for part-time workers as regards family allowances (June 1981), sickness and invalidity insurance (February and May 1982), occupational accident insurance (March 1982) and, most recently, unemployment insurance (March and July 1982, March 1983).

For workers employed irregularly, Egypt in 1980 introduced a special social security scheme which includes old-age, invalidity and survivors' benefits. Four million workers were covered by this scheme in June 1984.

The last example to be given here is that of France, where contractual arrangements complement the legislative provisions regarding temporary work (Law No. 72-1 of 3 January 1972, Ordinance No. 82-131 of 5 February 1982). An agreement was signed on 3 February 1983 concerning supplementary social security allowances in the event of sickness or accident.

As can be seen, in more and more countries broader and broader sectors of the economy, especially those employing large numbers of women, are now covered by social security schemes. This favourable development must, however, be followed up by revision of the relevant legislation, from which all discriminatory practices should be removed; only then will the principle of equal treatment for men and women become a reality. It is essential that all members of a social protection scheme should, irrespective of sex, be entitled to the same benefits for themselves and for their dependants. The conditions on which benefits are granted must be absolutely gender neutral. The same value must be attached to all contributions paid in by insured persons—men or women.

REMOVAL OF PROVISIONS WHICH DISCRIMINATE AGAINST WOMEN

Two broad trends can be distinguished in the efforts made by a number of States to rectify their social security legislation. In one, the aim is to guarantee to married women in employment the same rights as men regarding the benefits they can themselves claim by way of replacement income; in the other, it is to enable women workers, now that the traditional concept of the "head of the family" is losing ground, to acquire the same entitlements as men for the members of their families.

Personal rights of women workers

Most of the social security schemes in which coverage depends on the exercise of an occupation—in particular schemes for paid employees—are based on the principle of rights acquired in return for contributions paid; this applies both to the conditions of award and the methods of calculating benefits, and is independent of the worker's sex. However, traditional family patterns have left their mark as regards the entitlements a working wife can claim in her own right. The financial dependency which used to be the common lot of women is reflected in provisions which are now outdated, and in any case discriminatory. Any rights a married woman may have acquired through her own employment are denied her because of the protection she can obtain as a dependent person; in the most favourable of circumstances her rights may be recognised provided she meets certain conditions which are never required of men. In some schemes married women may not—in spite of the fact that they have been employed—qualify for benefits providing replacement income in certain contingencies.

Having lost their *raison d'être,* these discriminatory practices now appear to be contrary to the very principles on which social insurance was based. Several countries whose legislation included such differences in treatment have taken steps to correct the situation and to confer on women workers full status as insured persons in their own right, as will be seen from the following few examples.

Old-age and invalidity insurance

In the Federal Republic of Germany before 1968 insured women were allowed to seek reimbursement of their pension insurance contributions when they married. Many women availed themselves of this opportunity, which terminated their entitlement to a pension: in most cases they later regretted their decision. In 1982 a provision was implemented allowing them to pay back voluntarily the contributions which were returned to them, thereby re-establishing their entitlement; these voluntary contributions count towards the qualifying period for a pension.

In December 1979 the Netherlands amended its laws on general invalidity insurance and married women are now entitled to receive invalidity benefit. To begin with, the legislation excluded married women, although it did recognise some rights under certain conditions; 1 January 1979 was set as the date on which the new provisions would take effect. The Law of 20 December 1979 accorded benefits on the same terms to men and to all women, whether married or not. The legislation was thus brought into line with the 19 December 1978 Directive of the European Communities on the progressive implementation of the principle of equal treatment for men and women in matters of social security. In order to obtain invalidity benefit, the insured person—man or woman—must have suffered real loss of income, must have been gainfully occupied as a wage earner or a self-employed person during the course of the preceding year, and must have received at least a certain minimum income. A new law instituting equal treatment for men and women in the general old-age insurance scheme came into force in April 1985. Under the previous legislation a married women had no right to a pension on her own account; by virtue of the new law, she is personally entitled to her own pension. It should be noted that in occupational pension schemes, although women have equal access to membership (on the same conditions of age and length of service as men), the law, which dates from 1975, gives no guarantee of equal treatment.

In the United Kingdom since April 1978 (according to a 1975 law on social security pensions), married women in paid employment may no longer opt for limited coverage. Previously, they were allowed to pay very small contributions and to rely on their husbands' insurance for maternity benefits, retirement pensions (at a reduced rate) and death grants. Since 1978 women have enjoyed equality of access to occupational pension schemes as regards both age and the number of years' service required to become a member.

Unemployment insurance

In 1975 the United Kingdom did away with the lower rates for married women's unemployment allowances (and sickness benefit).

The new unemployment insurance plan introduced by Luxembourg in 1976 applies to married women in paid employment whose husbands have regular jobs at a normal wage.

Ireland has adopted several measures designed to reduce sex-based discrimination in unemployment benefits. As regards unemployment assistance (lump-sum payments), the rule that in order to obtain benefits a widow or a single woman had either to have dependants or to have paid 26 social insurance contributions was abolished in 1978. In April 1982 the scheme was extended to cover married women without dependants who are separated from their husbands. During the same period, in April 1979, the length of time during which unemployment insurance benefits (supplements to the earnings—related allowances) are paid to married women was increased from 156 to 312 days (it is 390 days for other beneficiaries).

Rights of family members

Protection for members of their families is an important element in the social coverage workers obtain by exercising their occupation. It is hardly fair that members of their families should be deprived of protection or should be subject to more stringent qualifying conditions just because the worker is a woman. Several countries have taken steps to eliminate any distinctions between men and in applying the notion of dependent spouse, in allocating survivors' benefits and in granting family allowances.

The notion of dependent spouse

In most social security schemes whose scope is defined in relation to the exercise of an occupation, in particular schemes for paid employees, a spouse who does not work is, in principle, presumed to be dependent on the spouse who does work, in the way that children are dependent. This fact of having a dependent spouse procures higher benefits for some of the risks faced by the insured person: invalidity, sickness, old age, unemployment. In many schemes the status of dependant is automatically attributed to all women who remain at home, without other qualifying conditions. Similar status, with its attendant rights, is rarely granted to the husband of a female employee and, when it is, the qualifying conditions are more stringent. This difference in treatment in effect reduces the value of the wife's contributions. Two examples follow which illustrate the changes taking place in this respect.

In Belgium a Royal Decree published on 16 May 1980 introduced new provisions concerning the definition of "dependent person", thereby putting the equal treatment principle into effect for mandatory insurance against sickness and invalidity. The traditional criteria of marital and paternal authority no longer apply. The spouse, male or female, who is not the holder of the insurance, or any other person who looks after the insurance holder's household without remuneration, is considered to be financially dependent.

In Austria, following a declaration by the Constitutional Court that any specific reference to gender in the general social insurance law was unconstitutional, the law was amended in July 1981 to provide equal treatment for men and women as far as benefits are concerned. Regarding sickness insurance, an insured wife can declare her uninsured husband to be her dependant, on condition that any income or pension he may receive does not exceed the amount laid down by law. The new legislation also extends protection to any person living with the insurance holder who runs the household.

Rights of the surviving spouse

In most countries the pension or annuity entitlements of a surviving spouse are not the same for widows as for widowers, or are at least not subject to the same conditions. Rarely, either in public schemes or in occupational schemes, does the wife's pension entitlement revert to her widower, either because there are no provisions to that effect or, more often, because the conditions to be met in practice exclude men from such benefits, except in the case of old age, invalidity or financial dependency. In other words, employed women who contribute towards a pension have no guarantee that after their deaths their husbands will be able to benefit from it, a fact which deprives them of one of the advantages of membership of such schemes and payment of the corresponding contributions.

A number of countries have amended their laws to ensure equal rights for men and women as regards the deceased spouse's pension entitlements, whenever this had not been written into the original rules. This is the case in Belgium, Canada, Denmark and (except for special or statutory schemes) France. In this field too, progress has come about as a result of changes in society, and instructive case-law decisions have been handed down in several countries.

In the Federal Republic of Germany the Federal Tribunal for Social Affairs, in its first decision on widowers' pensions, pointed out in 1963 that the roles of men and women within the family were such that it was doubtful that the family would suffer the same financial loss on the death of the wife as on the death of the husband. Consequently, there was some justification for making payment of a widower's pension contingent on the fact that he had been financially dependent on his late wife since legislators might assume, on the basis of traditional family structures, that the husband would not be left in need after the death of his spouse. In a second ruling in 1975 the same Tribunal recognised that the role of the married woman was changing and that a growing proportion of women were in paid employment. At the same time, however, it called attention to some particular features of women's working careers (shorter duration than those of men, lower remuneration) and, pointing out that only women in the younger age groups were affected by the current developments, declared that the legislation under attack was not yet entirely outdated, while calling on the legislators to see to it that it was overhauled.

These findings are a perfect illustration of the changes that have come about in most developed countries: the surviving spouse's entitlement to a pension originally stemmed from a state of dependency; in most cases the right to a widower's pension is still subject to an income test, but in future any financial conditions will have to be applied equitably to both men and women. The fact that a man who survives his spouse receives different treatment from that accorded to a woman in the same situation constitutes discrimination against married women in paid employment.

Taking a similar stand, in March 1977 the United States Supreme Court annulled the provision by virtue of which a widower was required to prove that at least half his living expenses were paid by his wife at the time of her death.

In July 1981 Austria recognised the right of men and women to equal treatment under its social insurance legislation, following the decision of the Constitutional Court, already mentioned, that any differences in the qualifying conditions for widows' and widowers' pensions were incompatible with the Constitution. The stricter qualifying conditions for widowers were annulled and the amount of widowers' pensions was to be gradually brought into line with that for widows' pensions, namely 60 per cent of the sponse's retirement pension. These adjustments were to apply in both the old-age and the occupational accident branches.

In Spain the Constitutional Court handed down rulings in November 1983 to the effect that any differences in treatment between men and women as regards the award of a pension to the surviving spouse—namely, the additional requirements of incapacity for work and financial dependence for the granting of a widower's pension—were incompatible with the Constitution, which strictly forbids any discrimination based on sex.

Benefits linked to the presence of children

Family allowances were designed to help families meet the expense of bringing up children and were introduced at a time when most married women did not work outside the home unless they were obliged to do so by financial need. The aim was to increase the resources of one-income families and to enable women to devote themselves entirely to their homes and children.

However, as the role of women in society has altered—as has the whole concept of marriage and the family—there has been a change in the purpose of family allowances. Their object now is to offset, at least in part, the expenditure incurred in connection with the maintenance and rearing of children. Nowadays, among other things, they help to cover the cost of child-minding for families where both parents are in paid employment. Neither automatic payment of these allowances to the father (in keeping with the old concept of his role as head of the family) nor systematic payment to the mother (as the traditional child-rearer) correspond to present-day reality, which requires a closer understanding of the life-style of today's family units. A number of countries have removed from their social security legislations any provisions which might be discriminatory in this respect.

In Sweden since 1976 children's supplements have been paid to recipients of social security pensions, whether father or mother; if both spouses receive pensions, the supplement is shared equally between them. In Ireland the household help allowance was extended to women in 1977; this allowance, which is paid when the presence of someone is needed in the home to look after the children, was previously available only to men.

In order to bring its legislation into line with the European Communities Directive of 19 December 1978 concerning the progressive implementation of the equal treatment principle in social security, the United Kingdom in 1980 passed a law giving married women who draw unemployment or sickness benefit the right, from November 1984 onwards, to receive children's supplements on the same terms as married men.

In Italy the Constitutional Court had occasion in July 1980 to make a ruling on equal treatment regarding children's allowances. The provision which was being contested stipulated that family allowances should be paid to the father even if both parents were gainfully employed. Pointing out that the Constitution guaranteed equality of treatment for all citizens, including husbands and wives, the Court held that no legislative provision could be based on the pre-eminence of the father or the husband within the family. It is worth noting that since the beginning of 1978 all family benefits have been available to women on the same conditions as men.

In Belgium the 1980 legislative changes concerning the concept of "dependent person" apply also to children. The notion of "head of the family" has been discarded. As regards sickness insurance, when both parents are working the children are presumed to be dependent on the older of the two, or on the parent entitled to the most extensive coverage. Children of separated or divorced parents are considered to be dependent on the parent who has been awarded physical custody.

In concluding this section on benefits linked to the presence of children, it is worth mentioning the new rules on old-age and survivors' insurance adopted in Switzerland in January 1983. Before that date, children of divorced mothers did not receive an orphan's allowance on her death unless she was responsible for maintaining them and was a member of an insurance scheme at the time of her death. These conditions, which did not apply to divorced fathers, have now been eliminated.

There is no doubt that the steps taken by States to widen the coverage of their social security systems and eliminate any provisions which discriminate against women have proved beneficial. In comparison with the situation faced by economically active women only ten or so years ago, much progress has been made. But this progress should not be allowed to mask the fact that a great deal remains to be done if the goal of equal treatment for men and women, as defined in this study, is to be achieved.

4 FURTHER CHANGES NEEDED

Despite the importance of the measures already adopted, national social security laws still contain many provisions which are unfair to women workers, both as regards the coverage provided by social security schemes and the machinery for awarding benefits. In this chapter, we give a general summary of the situation, before going on to examine in more detail the difficulties encountered in implementing the principle of equal treatment for men and women in social security, and the limitations circumscribing the principle itself in the present state of affairs. The few examples which follow serve only to illustrate the analysis and should in no circumstances be regarded as a complete catalogue of existing discrimination.

THE EXTENT OF SOCIAL COVERAGE FOR WOMEN

On the whole, workers employed in the private and public sectors are today well protected in all developed countries. They enjoy full social security coverage, either by virtue of universal schemes applicable to the entire population or through various schemes based on occupational activity. However, this favourable situation applies only to persons who are engaged in "normal" forms of regular, full-time employment. In most countries social legislation still makes little allowance for the atypical forms of paid work in which, as we have already noted, particularly large numbers of women are employed.

In the case of part-time employment, shorter working hours still often mean that workers are unable to take advantage of the provisions of social security legislation. It is even more difficult for them than for full-time workers to complete the qualifying period which governs the award of benefits and possibly the amounts to be awarded. The qualifying conditions for coverage of unemployment risks and access to supplementary retirement pension schemes in many cases exclude part-time workers, or at least those among them who work less than a fixed number of hours. Thus, in Australia and New Zealand, part-time employees are not eligible for unemployment benefit. In Japan only those who work at least three-quarters of the normal working hours are eligible for unemployment insurance, and in the Federal Republic of Germany and the Netherlands only those working at least half time. In addition to such differences in treatment, in some countries part-time workers are simply excluded from supplementary pension schemes as, for instance, in Canada.

Work carried out in the home, where the use of automatic data processing techniques and telematics have opened up entirely new fields, is still poorly protected everywhere. Few efforts are being made, even today, to adapt social security legislation to such cases. In various countries, Italy and Norway for example, the conditions on which unemployment benefits are granted result in the exclusion of women homeworkers.

Another form of work in which social security systems discriminate against women is participation in family businesses. As has already been pointed out, social security programmes are beginning to recognise such joint efforts and protection is already being offered in several countries. However, there is still a long way to go before all the implications of the situation—which is after all an employment relationship—are fully recognised. Frequently the women in question are insured through their husband's activity, which means that when they are unable to work because of illness, maternity or accident they are not entitled to receive any allowances; nor do they acquire any personal entitlement to old-age benefits.

In the developing countries the overall trend between 1975 and 1985 was towards the strengthening and improvement of existing social security schemes; the changes have, therefore, mainly benefited wage earners, in both the private and public sectors. These developments are of special importance to women working in the public sector since, given the improvements in women's education, more and more of them are entering such employment, as in the industrialised countries.

This being said, whole sectors of the economy still lack any form of social protection. In many countries, for instance, nothing has yet been done for the agricultural sector, although large numbers of the population, both male and female, work on the land. The position of self-employed workers too is often precarious, except when, as in a few countries, protection schemes based solely on residence have been introduced.

QUALIFYING CONDITIONS

Since they occur mainly in sectors and forms of activity which employ a high proportion of women, gaps in protection tend to perpetuate inequality of treatment for women workers. Moreover, even when women are included in the protected population, social security schemes only too often still contain provisions which discriminate against them.

In identifying any cases of discrimination which still exist in national social security legislation, we propose, with the help of several examples which we consider to be important, to follow the general plan of analysis adopted by Colette Même in her report (already referred to) on the implementation within the European Communities of the principle of equal treatment for men and women in social security.[1] For each of the subjects dealt with, we shall examine the justifications put forward for differences in treatment, and consider what should be done about the resulting inequalities.

Concerning the conditions for access to certain benefits, social security schemes often, as we have already said, include provisions which apply to women workers only. Some of these are manifestly unfavourable in that they in fact contest or diminish the value of women's contributions. Others are more ambiguous and are often meant to offset the handicaps women experience in acquiring their own individual entitlements. Lastly, there is another category of provisions which call for close scrutiny; these are not openly directed at women and, at first sight, would appear to be sex neutral.

Manifestly discriminatory provisions

Acquisition of rights

Although in most social insurance schemes the sex of the worker in no way affects his or her obligation to pay contributions, in a few cases discrimination against women begins even at this early stage. The amount of the contribution to be paid is sometimes based on certain characteristics of the person to be insured; the result may be that some of those affiliated to the scheme may have to pay considerably more than others.

This method is mainly applied to women seeking to enter private supplementary schemes. In Canada, for instance, the actuarial rates for private pension schemes are calculated for men and women separately, rather than for all contributors on the basis of overall mortality tables which are not differentiated by sex, a method which would spread the risks evenly over all participants. The result is that women have to pay higher contributions than men.

Sickness and maternity insurance in Switzerland offers a further example of unequal treatment. Contributions are calculated according to the actual cost of providing benefits for each group of insured persons, classified

[1] *La mise en œuvre de l'égalité de traitement entre hommes et femmes en matière de sécurité sociale en ce qui concerne les prestations non soumises à la Directive 79/7/EEC du 19 décembre 1978: inventaire et propositions,* Definitive synthesis report by Ms. C. Même, doc. V/1261/84-FR (Brussels, Commission of the European Communities, July 1984).

by sex, age at admission and the cost of care. This means that women may be required to pay sums which are 10 per cent higher than the corresponding male contributions.

The existence of these and similar provisions constitutes a serious infringement of the equal treatment principle. In the United States their discriminatory nature has been condemned in a court of law. The case in question concerned a public sector pension scheme which required women to pay 15 per cent more than men, because of the difference in life expectancy between the sexes. In November 1976 the court trying the case found that, since it had not been proved that each individual woman had a longer expectation of life than the male life expectancy rate, and since factors other than sex which could affect longevity had not been taken into account, the differences in contribution rates constitued unjustified discrimination. The same case then came before the Supreme Court which, basing its judgement on the spirit and the letter of the law on equal employment opportunities, according to which any act of discrimination against an individual on the grounds of sex is illegal, in April 1978 found that, even though a particular characteristic might be attributed to a category of persons, this did not justify any act which might cause prejudice to an individual in whom the characteristic could not be demonstrated. The position of the United States legal authorities is clear: in the acquisition of individual entitlements, no one may be the object of discriminatory measures based on a statistical particularity of the group to which he or she belongs, since there can be no proof, *a priori,* that the person in question will develop that particularity. This applies in particular to any sex-based discrimination, which is forbidden by law.

Discriminatory conditions of admission are also to be found in supplementary pension schemes. In Belgium, more often than not, supplementary old-age insurance is only voluntary for women workers but compulsory for their male colleagues. In Switzerland married women are not always admitted to the optional supplementary schemes which cover 80 per cent of male employees, or are admitted on conditions which differ from those applied to men. These are only two examples of discrimination against women in this field.

Whereas in many social security schemes qualifying conditions are identical for women and for men, women do not enjoy identical entitlement to benefits, either on their own behalf or on behalf of their families.

Personal rights acquired by women workers

Married women who are economically active are often treated differently from men in social security schemes. The idea that a woman is dependent on her husband is still in evidence in old-age and unemployment insurance in particular.

Old-age insurance

In some old-age insurance schemes the couple is invariably taken to be the economic unit whose existence gives rise to the payment of a single inclusive pension, even though both spouses have been in paid employment. In Switzerland, for instance, the old-age pension paid to a couple is 150 per cent of the pension paid to a single person. In the Netherlands, before the recent reform of the old-age pension scheme, it was the husband's age (65) which determined the date from which a married couple's pension became due. The couple received an amount equivalent to 100 per cent of the minimum guaranteed income, the rate for single persons being 70 per cent. Since the reform, each partner is personally entitled to a pension equal to 50 per cent of the minimum guaranteed income.

Unemployment insurance

Some unemployment insurance schemes make a clear distinction between men and women as regards entitlement to benefits. In Ireland, in spite of recent progress, the only women who can claim unemployment insurance benefits are single women or women with dependent families, and even then the allowances are lower than those granted to married men in the same situation. In the Netherlands, under the scheme which provides unemployment allowances for workers who have been unemployed for six months or longer, married women are not entitled to benefits unless they can prove that they are the family's second bread-winner.

Such discriminatory practices would appear to be vestiges of a situation in which the occupational activities of women were considered to be of only minor importance. The changing role of women in economic and social life and the emergence of a new concept of the "couple" have done much to make this attitude obsolete.

Rights of family members

The assumption that a wife is financially dependent on her husband, which in many cases serves as the basis for recognition of her derived entitlements and for the higher benefits her husband receives by way of dependents' allowances, hardly applies when the wife is the main insurance holder. The discriminatory nature of this assumption has become even more apparent during the past decade or two, now that more and more women are gainfully employed.

Persistence of the notion of family bread-winner

In many schemes the wife still has to prove that she is the family bread-winner before her dependants can claim any entitlements deriving from her insurance. This applies, inter alia, to health care in Belgium, France, the Federal Republic of Germany, Ireland, Italy, Luxembourg and the Netherlands.

The same condition often applies to the increments paid for any dependants. In France and Italy, where invalidity pensions may be increased during hospital stays when the person in question has a family to support, a married woman must prove that she is the main source of family income before she can claim the higher amount. In the Federal Republic of Germany, Luxembourg and the United Kingdom, where a supplement to the invalidity pension is paid when there are dependent children, the wife again has to prove that she is the family bread-winner. In Greece, in the old-age pension branch of the scheme applying to the agricultural sector, a monthly dependant's allowance is paid for wives but not for husbands: in the other schemes, the allowance is paid automatically for wives but for husbands only if they are disabled or in need.

Such provisions fail to take account of situations—and nowadays they are very frequent—in which both spouses are employed and both are covered by social insurance. Protection—for health insurance in particular—may be more extensive for one spouse than for the other: it would appear only fair that dependants should be able to take advantage of the fuller insurance, whatever the sex of the holder. Furthermore, in everyday circumstances it is the mother who more often than not advances the money needed to pay medical expenses, for the children in particular; it is therefore only right that she should be reimbursed personally. Lastly, it is not unusual these days for a woman actually to provide for her family's material needs, either because the couple has broken up or because the husband is not, or is no longer, employed. The logical conclusion is, then, that dependants should be entitled to a derived entitlement whatever the sex of the insured person, and that any increments should accrue and be paid either to the spouse actually maintaining the dependant or dependants, or to whichever of the spouses is nominated by mutual consent.

Rights of the surviving spouse

In most social security legislations there are still considerable differences between the entitlements of widowers and those accorded to widows.

Some schemes make no provision for reversion to the widower of any of his deceased wife's pension or annuity entitlements. This is true for agricultural workers in Greece and in the special schemes for seafarers and mineworkers in France.

Other schemes apply stricter qualifying conditions to widowers than to widows, as will be seen from the following examples.

In Luxembourg a widower is only entitled to a pension on the death of his wife if she was the family bread-winner. In the Netherlands such pensions are paid to the widower only if he suffers from a work disability of 50 per cent or more and his wife provided the family income. These two conditions—incapacity for work and financial dependence—exist in many other countries: in Cameroon in the scheme covering wage earners and in Malaysia (both conditions), in Tunisia in the agricultural sector (invalidity) and in Uruguay (total incapacity for work, lack of any means of subsistence and financial dependence at the time of the wife's death). In the United Kingdom the survivors' benefits paid in the occupational accidents and diseases branch are granted to a widower only if, at the time of his wife's death, he was permanently incapable of providing for his own needs and if the deceased wife contributed more than 50 per cent of his upkeep. In the German Democratic Republic the pension entitlement reverts to the widower only at the age of 65, whereas the widow is entitled to a survivors' pension at the age of 60.

The fact that in the developed countries widows receive more favourable treatment than widowers is a legacy from the times when very few women enjoyed financial independence. Elsewhere, it is a way of compensating for the absence of protection for women, who are still only too often excluded from social insurance schemes by their limited scope and by the terms and conditions of female employment. Today it would seem only fair that identical contributions to insurance schemes should produce identical results, irrespective of the contributor's sex. Similarly, more thought should be given to the state of poverty in which a man whose wife was providing his material needs may find himself after her death.

With the exception of work injuries, it would appear that no scheme pays a survivor's pension on the sole condition of death of the spouse; other conditions are applied, either separately or in conjunction: age, duration of the marriage, the presence of children, and so on. The granting of a pension is motivated by the existence of a "dependency link" and by the financial "vulnerability" of the surviving spouse: there is a desire to protect the aged, those who have never worked or who have not worked long enough to acquire the right to a pension large enough to live on, as well as those who lack the capacity to work (in the broadest sense of the expression).

From the point of view of principle, there is no longer any justification for granting such protection to women only: it could be extended to cover men in similar situations, which would fulfil the dual purpose of ending a state of affairs which discriminates against women workers and improving the position of certain widowers who find themselves in difficult financial circumstances. Should such a change be introduced, it could perhaps be accompanied by a tightening up of the qualifying conditions for receipt of a widow's pension. A survivor's pension would then be granted only to a spouse, male or female, who was actually dependent on the deceased person and who, by reason of age or state of health, is unable to exercise an occupation.

Benefits linked to the presence of children

Discriminatory provisions exist in this branch—when only the mother works or when both spouses work—both as regards the conditions for the award of benefits and the manner in which they are paid.

Some schemes still require women to prove their status as head of the family before they can draw family allowances. In the public employees' scheme in force in Luxembourg, female workers are entitled to receive benefits only if the husband is unable to work or if his income is lower than the agreed "social minimum", whereas benefits are paid automatically to male employees.

When both parents meet the conditions for receipt of benefits, some legislations give priority to the father—in Belgium, for instance—and others to the mother—Ireland, the Netherlands and the United Kingdom. These priorities may not always be neutral as, for example, when the two spouses enjoy different entitlements under different schemes.

The recipient, that is to say the person who actually receives the benefit, often varies according to the regulations in force. Sometimes the allowance is paid to the father, as for example in Belgium (in the self-employed workers' scheme), the Federal Republic of Germany, Luxembourg, the Netherlands and Switzerland, and sometimes to the mother, even though the entitlement has been acquired as a result of the father's activity. This is the case in Belgium (for wage-earners), Denmark, Greece, Ireland and the United Kingdom.

The reasons put forward for these differences in treatment would no longer appear to be valid. Provisions which favour the father often derive from the fact that family allowances were—and sometimes still are—advanced by the employer and paid out together with wages. But today the quality of wage earner is no longer a specifically male attribute.

As to the provisions which are more favourable to women, they are mainly based on recognition of women's role in child rearing. But changes in family life-styles in industrialised countries are gradually leading to a new distribution of tasks between men and women. Although they have not yet reached all countries, such changes, related as they are to the spread of female employment, call for the elimination here and now of all differences of treatment in the attribution and remittance of all benefits intended for children.

When both parents are eligible for benefits, the fairest solution would be to let them decide who should receive them or, if the couple no longer exists, to confer the entitlement on the parent who actually maintains the children. Similar arrangements would apply to the actual payment of the allowances.

Differences in treatment presented as favourable to women

In the old-age branch many countries have introduced special provisions which make allowance for the constraints that often hamper women in their employment. The first of the two types of provision that we shall be examining in this section of the study affects mothers; the second is of concern to all women.

Taking into consideration the time spent raising children

Many old-age insurance schemes include provisions intended to offset the handicap in acquiring pension credits suffered by economically active women when they interrupt their work to bring up children, thereby reducing their contribution period. These provisions apply mainly to women in paid employment and are mostly to be found in occupation-based schemes in developed countries, where large numbers of women work outside the home.

In addition to the general possibilities for taking out voluntary insurance during non-working periods or the retroactive payment of contributions, many legislations make special arrangements for mothers wishing to acquire a pension entitlement. We shall examine these provisions—more flexible qualifying periods, free prolongation of the insured period, and others—in Part Two of this study (Chapter 6, "The development of personal rights for women"). Here we shall consider them only from the point of view of equal treatment. The fact is that such opportunities are open either to mothers only or, much less frequently, to both fathers and mothers but with more restrictive conditions for the former.

One question that springs to mind is to what extent countries are justified in granting such rights automatically, as is often the case. Whereas it is conceivable that a period during which work is interrupted should be taken into account for insurance purposes, there is less justification for doing so when only mothers reap the benefit, simply because they are mothers. Moreover, any advantages offered in this way should depend on the actual duration of the drop-out period. And do not such measures help to promote motherhood as a vocation for women, thus leading to inequality vis-à-vis employment? From the "career" point of view, the favourable aspects are less obvious. In any event, the first consideration is that they should not be allowed to continue unless they also apply to fathers; it might, for instance, be possible to leave any decision in the matter to the parents themselves.

Retirement age

Many legislations treat men and women differently when it comes to the age at which they are entitled to old-age pensions; usually women become eligible at an earlier age than men. The difference is generally five years: this is the case in almost half the OECD countries and in the countries of Eastern Europe (with the exception of Czechoslovakia, where it is three years), and in numerous developing countries.[2]

The arrangements for early retirement in force in several countries either confirm or reinforce the difference in treatment accorded to working mothers. In Bulgaria and the USSR, for instance, the age of entitlement to a pension is lowered by five years for mothers who have brought up five children. In the German Democratic Republic it is lowered by one year for every child up to a limit of four years.

The texts applying to workers carrying out arduous tasks also often make special provision for women. In Poland, for example, Ordinance No. 100 concerning the retirement age for manual workers, which took effect on 1 August 1978, maintains a lower age for women.

Various reasons have been put forward to justify these differences. Earlier retirement could help to compensate for the "double work-day" that many women have to put up with. It could meet the wishes of some women to start drawing a pension at the same time as their husbands, who are often older than they are. Another reason given is that women experience more difficulty in finding new jobs once they have passed a certain age. None of these explanations appears fully convincing today. If—to take the provisions concerning certain types of work—the arduousness of an occupation is such that it justifies a lower retirement age, this should apply to all workers in that occupation, irrespective of sex.

Conversely, one might ask whether a lower retirement age really is an advantage for women. The effect is to shorten their working lives and, since they often receive lower wages than men, earlier retirement is more in the nature of a handicap. It should also be borne in mind that, in times of economic recession, considerable pressure is put on workers who are entitled to a pension to give up their jobs: women are thus the first to be excluded from the workforce.

Discrimination between men and women with regard to retirement age has drawn sharp criticism in several countries.

In the United States plans to fix a lower pensionable age for women than for men have been condemned as discriminatory. The reforms approved by Congress in 1983, which provide for a gradual raising of the retirement age from 65 to 67 by the year 2027, contain no provisions referring specifically to women. In the United Kingdom the Equal Opportunities Commission in 1978 proposed a compromise solution. Instead of 60 for women and 65 for men, pensionable age would be set at 63 for all: this suggestion has provoked a lively nation-wide debate.

---

[2] "Social security and the elderly: Background document prepared for the World Assembly on Aging by the International Social Security Association", in *International Social Security Review* (Geneva, ISSA), 1982, No. 4, pp. 489 et seq.

National courts of law have also been called up on to state their views, and the findings of the Japanese and Italian courts are worth quoting.

In March 1975 the Tokyo High Court found the arrangement whereby men retired at the age of 55 and women at 50 unacceptable: it was unjustified, discriminatory towards women, and for this reason was contrary both to the law of the land and to good practice. In August of the same year the Supreme Court found to be discriminatory in terms of both the Constitution and the country's labour laws a clause in a contract concluded between a travel agency and its employees which required women to leave their jobs at an earlier age than their male colleagues.

In Italy the Court of Cassation in December 1981 declared any clause in a work contract which obliged women to retire earlier than men, thereby hampering the progress of their careers and making it more difficult for them to obtain various benefits, to be illegal and incompatible with the country's Constitution. Under the terms of Law 903 of 9 December 1977 regarding equal treatment for men and women in employment, women who meet the old-age pension qualifying conditions may choose to continue working up to the normal retirement age for men, provided they give their employers three months' notice of their decision.

The solution adopted by the Italian law-makers brings up the question of how to eliminate differences in treatment between men and women as regards the age of entitlement to an old-age pension. Should the retirement age for women be raised to match that of men, should the pensionable age for men be lowered to that of women, or should the age for both sexes be somewhere in between the two? This is a sensitive question, the answer to which depends both on the limitations imposed by the overall economic circumstances and on the financial constraints weighing on pension schemes themselves, the two of which have to be reconciled as far as possible. Looking ahead, the very notion of a fixed retirement age has come in for criticism. Some experts in the matter recommend the introduction of a flexible system, with a period of transition between full working life and retirement, and identical qualifying conditions for all—a solution which would eliminate any provisions that discriminate against women workers.

Indirect discrimination

The provisions we shall be examining in this section—to be referred to as indirect discrimination— are at least as frequent as those already mentioned; but they are more insidious, less clear-cut and call for careful investigation. Their discriminatory character stems less from their intrinsic nature than from the situations in which they apply. Although they are not openly based on sex, the resulting differences in treatment nevertheless work to the detriment of women.

The first problem is to identify such provisions and to demonstrate their discriminatory nature, in spite of their apparent neutrality. Here we shall provide three brief examples, taken from labour case-law, which illustrate the procedure followed by the courts in detecting and penalising indirect discrimination; a similar method might well be used in assessing respect for the principle of equal treatment in social security.

In the United Kingdom a firm which was reducing its staff had intended first to dismiss its part-time workers—who were mostly women—before applying a length-of-service criterion to its full-time employees. The case was brought before an appeals court which in September 1982 found that to take into account length of service for full-time workers only constituted, in this instance, unlawful discrimination against women.

In an enterprise operating in the Federal Republic of Germany workers on the night shift were receiving a bonus for night work, a second bonus which was higher than the corresponding bonus for workers on the day shift, plus an additional allowance known as the "labour market bonus" designed, according to the management, to attract candidates for night work. This additional allowance was not, therefore, a bonus for actual night work, but only those working on the night shift could claim it; in practice this meant that only men were eligible, since women are forbidden by law to engage in night work. The Federal Court found in January 1983: firstly that there should be no difference between the bonuses paid to day workers and those paid to night workers if, in addition, a special bonus was paid for night work; secondly, that it was up to the enterprise to prove that the additional "labour market allowance" was indispensable in recruiting workers for the night shift. Otherwise, the payment of such an allowance could constitute *de facto* discrimination against women.

For its part, the Court of Justice of the European Communities was consulted in 1981 on a complicated question of indirect discrimination stemming from the fact that hourly rates of pay were lower for part-time workers than for full-time workers and that most of the part-time workers were women, who thus earned 10 per cent less per hour than men employed full time.[3] The Court found that the payment of a lower hourly rate to part-time employees was not in itself discriminatory, but that it could become so if there was no objective justification for it.

In tracking down indirect discrimination, it is not so much the legislative, regulatory or contractual provisions themselves which are at fault, but the practical aspects of their application: it is no longer enough to refer to the law as such; it is the *de facto* situation which must be taken into account. The foregoing court findings reveal that indirect social discrimination exists when conditions are set for which there is no objective justification—conditions which a smaller proportion of women than men can meet and which, therefore, cause prejudice to female workers.

There are in social security legislations certain qualifying conditions which, although they make no specific reference to sex, in practice penalise

[3] Jenkins v. Kinsgate.

women. In New Zealand, for example, unemployment insurance benefits are payable only if the household income is less than a given amount; the result is that married women who are gainfully employed but whose earnings are not the family's main source of income rarely receive such benefits. In Canada, where private pension plans make no provision for the transfer of pension credits, the situation is particularly disadvantageous to women who, more often than men, take up short-term employment or leave their jobs to follow their spouses. This means that it is mainly women who draw no benefit from clauses guaranteeing the maintenance of pension entitlements, which apply to persons over the age of 45 who have worked at least ten years for the same employer (in fact, women contribute on behalf of men).

Such instances are to be found in, and such conclusions can be drawn for, all social security schemes that impose conditions which are neutral in appearance but which are far more difficult for women to satisfy than men.

One of the greatest difficulties in social security is to distinguish between situations which really do constitute indirect discrimination, that is, which have their origins in social security provisions as such, and those which reflect pre-existing inequalities—unequal remuneration, for instance. There is no doubt that elimination of the first of these is a task for social security administrations and should be one of the main objectives of national social policies. As to the second, it is not the work of social security legislators to compensate for the pre-existing inequalities which both characterise the status of women and derive from that status.

DIFFICULTIES IN APPLYING THE PRINCIPLE OF EQUAL TREATMENT

A definition of occupational activity which is out of touch with the realities of women's work, together with today's unfavourable socio-economic climate, hamper at this time the implementation of the principle of equal treatment for men and women in social security.

Definition of occupational activity

In most countries membership of a social security scheme depends on the exercise of an occupational activity. The trouble is that some activities exercised almost entirely by women are totally excluded from the definition of "employment"; activities which differ from strictly household tasks, which take up a good deal of women's time—sometimes outside their homes—and require certain skills or aptitudes but which, because they are not paid, deny those exercising them the status of "worker", by the same token depriving them of the right to join a social security scheme.

This situation is detrimental to women on at least two counts. The exercise of such an activity, which is rarely the result of a completely free choice, makes it impossible for them to take up "real" paid employment which would entitle them to their own social security coverage. What is more, the undeniable contribution made by women engaged in such activities receives no recognition from society, the only status accorded to these "second-class" workers being that of a "dependent person".

The activities in question, which are not really housework yet are not regarded as true occupations, and which remain outside the scope of social security systems, are carried out in various forms by women all over the world.

In rural areas of the developing countries they include the many agricultural tasks performed by women, which often provide the family with its principal means of subsistence, and various other activities which are grafted on to womens' traditional domestic duties, such as the processing and packaging of agricultural produce, weaving, and so on. In the towns they include the many jobs performed by women in the informal sector, where the labour force is largely female. These activities are for the most part absent from the statistics compiled by the usual census methods and are ignored when it comes to social security coverage. The social protection of large numbers of women depends on recognition of this type of activity; in many countries such protection would require extension of the coverage provided by already existing schemes.

Another field in which the work of large numbers of women is totally unappreciated is that of assistance to persons in need of care and attention. Here the inequality of treatment is particularly striking in the industrially developed countries where, in other sectors, much progress has been made towards the recognition of women's contribution to the economy—even when they are not paid. These caring activities are by no means of minor importance; in 1982 the Equal Opportunities Commission in the United Kingdom estimated at 1.25 million the number of persons, mainly women, who in that country were caring in their homes for old, sick or handicapped people incapable of looking after themselves. Such work is both physically and psychologically exhausting and results in forced withdrawal from the labour market with all the attendant consequences as regards income and social protection. Rarely estimated at its true value, this unpaid work—which is essentially carried out by women—is not classified as employment and, in almost all cases, provides no social security protection whatever.[4]

Present definitions of employment and the methods currently used for the collection of labour market statistics provide only an incomplete picture

---

[4] United Kingdom, Equal Opportunities Commission: *Caring for the elderly and the handicapped: Community care policies and women's lives* (Manchester, Mar. 1982); idem: *Who cares for the carers? Opportunities for those caring for the elderly and handicapped* (Manchester, Mar. 1982).

of women's work. Although apparently clear in theory, the distinction drawn between a woman's tasks "at work" and those carried out "in the home" in fact distort the realities of women's work.

An unfavourable socio-economic situation

Underlying the inequalities of treatment in social security, as regards both access to protection and the allocation of benefits, are a multitude of economic and social distortions which affect women at all stages and in all aspects of their working lives. These are the consequence of unequal access to training, the undervaluation of women's work, mental resistance to the progress achieved in female employment—sometimes in defiance of the law—and the persistence of a particular concept of women's place in society.

Given the nature and the extent of the discrimination which still exists, it is absolutely essential that comprehensive, coherent strategies be adopted in favour of women in all branches of social legislation. Social security programmes can be made to serve many different purposes and States can use benefits to various ends. This situation has a marked effect on women in that the specially adapted social protection offered to them is often a means of achieving aims which have nothing to do with a desire for equal treatment, such as, for instance, raising the birth rate, stimulating some sectors of the economy or persuading women to leave the labour force.

In time of economic recession, the promotion of equal rights for women is, unfortunately, not a priority. In the absence of a unanimous political will to achieve equality, it is essential to keep a careful watch on any "spontaneous" developments which may arise from the generally unfavourable economic climate. For instance, the growth of "atypical" forms of employment for women, part-time work in particular, whose drawbacks as regards social protection have already been pointed out, helps to keep women workers in a position of inferiority and to confine them to certain branches of activity, and has an unfavourable effect on their remuneration. Moreover, it changes peoples' attitudes to the sharing of domestic tasks and encourages a return to a more traditional division of labour between husband and wife, which can make it more difficult for women to return to a full-time job.

There can, of course, be no question of restricting the growth of part-time work just because of the danger it represents for women's occupational and social status—jobs offering "à la carte" working hours are bound to spread—but this form of activity must receive full recognition so that the workers concerned can be better protected. In order to reduce the risk of discrimination, more part-time jobs must be offered, part-time work must not be dominated by women, social protection schemes must be redesigned and trade unions must be persuaded to give more thought to the specific problems of part-time employees, both male and female.

More generally speaking, the harmonious development of female employment, and of the social protection which should go along with it, depends on resolute, concerted policies designed to enhance training opportunities for women, both initial training and refresher courses, to improve the working woman's image in the eyes of the world and to encourage the sharing of family responsibilities. In a future which is still difficult to foresee, only identical attitudes to the occupational activities of men and women will ensure strictly equal social rights for both sexes.

In the meantime, is full equality between men and women in social security matters to be regarded as an end in itself which must be achieved in its entirety, or are there still some specifically female aspects of employment which justify differences of treatment in social security schemes?

It would seem that the scope for implementation of the equal treatment principle varies over time and according to location. In places where the financial situation of women, even of women workers, remains precarious and female employment remains unstable, it would appear only fair and desirable to maintain certain provisions which apply only to women, in particular provisions concerning benefits which are linked to the status of dependent person. On the other hand, in places where an irreversible development of female employment and enhanced career opportunities for women make it possible, differences of treatment between men and women must be permanently eradicated, at least as regards future generations, especially when such differences incite women, even indirectly, to give up their work—be it only temporarily. If there is a need for special measures in favour of women, they should be designed in such a way as to help women overcome the difficulties they experience in obtaining employment; a whole series of integrated measures to combat unemployment and promote vocational training for women wishing to enter or re-enter the labour force must be not only maintained but considerably reinforced.

The foregoing comments provide a critical assessment of the progress already accomplished in implementing the principle of equal treatment, and of the outlook for the future. As the analysis has shown, it is still necessary at this time to provide social protection especially designed to meet women's specific requirements; but there is also a need to seek new solutions which keep pace with the changes taking place in modern societies.

PART TWO

THE CONTINUING NEED FOR SPECIFIC PROTECTION FOR WOMEN

Having examined the situation of women workers vis-à-vis social security, it is now necessary to consider the position of women who are temporarily or habitually inactive. Taking the traditional point of view, one can look at social protection for women from two angles: the specific protection they receive during maternity, and the protection they receive in various other contingencies as the wives of insured persons or as mothers. It is worth while taking a look at the ways in which such protection is being adjusted to take account of the increasing uniformity of roles within society and the efforts made by women to secure better social coverage for themselves. These developments have resulted in the emergence of the notion of "worker with family responsibilities". They have also led to a demand for personal entitlement to social coverage for women which is independent of their financial or marital status. At the same time, the will to fight poverty has brought with it policies which are more specifically designed to help women.

FROM MATERNITY PROTECTION TO THE PROTECTION OF WORKERS WITH FAMILY RESPONSIBILITIES

5

Since 1975 considerable improvements have taken place in the protection of women at the time of maternity. There are various reasons for this, the main ones being the enhanced role women now play in the production process and the efforts they themselves have made to improve their position in society. Recognition of the principle that women should enjoy equal status within the social framework (for instance, that they should have an equal right to work) is characteristic of the period. The desire to implement this principle has led governments to seek structures which would allow women to reconcile their economic activities with their family responsibilities, the more so since there have been profound demographic changes with, in particular, a drop in birth rates in the industrially developed countries. At the same time, female economic activity rates, including the activity rates for married women with children, have risen. Changing habits have affected attitudes to marriage. Falling birth rates have been accompanied by a rise in age at marriage and higher divorce rates, the result being an increase in the number of "unstable" families and of single parents.

Social security has adjusted to this new situation, inter alia, by developing the notion of "workers with family responsibilities", and by broadening the scope of what was once defined as "maternity protection"; in so doing it addresses the problems of both men and women equally, by promoting the spread of collective child-care facilities and making it easier for fathers and mothers with dependent children to take jobs.

MATERNITY PROTECTION AS SUCH

From 1975 to 1985 there was a general trend towards better protection for women during pregnancy and the post-natal period. This has resulted in improved benefits in kind and maternity grants which, as part of the overall campaign to improve public health, are now increasingly accorded to all women. In many countries considerable progress has been made as regards the duration of maternity leave and payment during such leave for women workers, whose right to keep their jobs is also better protected. After a brief reminder of the standards adopted by the International Labour Organisation, we shall go on to examine the provisions introduced in various countries.

ILO standards

The International Labour Conference has adopted two Conventions concerning the protection of women before and after childbirth—the Maternity Protection Convention, 1919 (No. 3), and the Maternity Protection Convention (Revised), 1952 (No. 103).

Convention No. 3, which applies to all women employed in industrial and commercial undertakings, provides for 12 weeks' maternity leave, to be taken in two parts, one before and the other after childbirth, the latter being compulsory. It recognises the woman's right to benefits sufficient for maintenance of herself and her child, to be paid either out of public funds or by means of a system of insurance, and her right to receive free medical care. This Convention also makes it unlawful for an employer to give a woman notice of dismissal during her maternity leave or during any period of sickness resulting from pregnancy or delivery. It provides for breaks during the working day to allow her to breast-feed her child.

Recommendation No. 12 (1921) on the protection of maternity for agricultural workers calls on member States to take steps to ensure that women in paid agricultural employment receive protection before and after childbirth similar to that contained in Convention No. 3.

The provisions of Convention No. 3 are taken up again in more detail in Convention No. 103. This Convention is also broader in its scope, in that it applies to all women employed in industrial and non-industrial undertakings and to women in agricultural occupations, including women wage earners working at home. In addition to stipulating, as does Convention No. 3, that a woman should receive benefits sufficient to maintain herself and her child, it fixes the rate of cash payments at not less than two-thirds of previous earnings.

Recommendation No. 95, which complements Convention No. 103, recommends that maternity leave be extended to a total period of 14 weeks, that cash payments be equal to 100 per cent of the woman's previous earnings, that she should receive certain supplementary benefits and more extensive medical care, that her job be protected for a longer period, that steps be taken to safeguard the health of pregnant women and new mothers (certain tasks known to be prejudicial to the mother's health are prohibited and she is entitled to a transfer to another kind of work which is not harmful), and that facilities for nursing mothers be provided.

Benefits in kind and maternity grants

Benefits in kind

In the movement towards generalised sickness and maternity insurance or national health services, the main emphasis is on medical care for women before, during and after childbirth. Most countries which possess the necessary facilities now cover the cost of care and hospital treatment during pregnancy, confinement and the post-natal period, either through social security or through their health services.

Although there is no need to repeat here all the examples of improved social coverage already mentioned in Part One of this study, it is worth noting that in Gabon protection was extended to all nationals in 1983 and now includes the cost of confinement. In Peru a law enacted in 1979 introduced into the social insurance system health benefits (medical care, pharmaceuticals) for all insured women and for all women covered by another person's insurance. In Nicaragua the March 1982 law which set up the National Health Service introduced free medical care and free medication during maternity for wives and common-law wives of insured men. The same arrangement existed in Guatemala before 1980. In Costa Rica since August 1980 maternity care has been guaranteed for the daughters of insured persons. In short, public health and public assistance policies have played a more important role in maternity protection than the introduction or extension of social security schemes in those areas of Africa, Asia and Latin America where such schemes are not very highly developed.

In countries or regions with more advanced social security systems, progress has been made by extending coverage to occupational categories which were not previously included. In Hungary, for example, maternity benefits have since 1983 been granted to wives whose husbands manage small enterprises under contract. More generally speaking, medical benefits in kind are now being accorded to residents (*de jure* or *de facto*), without other qualifying conditions. Thus, the requirements concerning prior affiliation to an insurance scheme were relaxed in France in 1980 and abolished in Luxembourg in 1983. Similarly, in the Federal Republic of Germany mothers have since 1979 been entitled to the benefits of social protection during the six months following childbirth even though they may not have paid any prior contributions. In Finland a 1981 law guarantees free medical care during maternity on the basis of residence alone, as in most Nordic countries.

As part of their public health policies, some countries have introduced regular medical check-ups (usually free of charge) for pregnant women and small children. Many countries have initiated preventive programmes based on vaccination, medical examination of children and health education. It is worth noting that in some cases this concern for health may go hand in hand with a desire to lower birth rates. In the Republic of Korea certain restrictions were introduced in 1983: insured women are no longer entitled to maternity benefits from the third child onwards, although medical care is still provided if there are complications.

Maternity grants

In many countries social security schemes provide lump-sum cash benefits or benefits in kind on the birth of a child to help cover the cost or to supply certain needs connected with the birth (maternity grants, pre-natal or post-natal allowances, milk or layette coupons, and the like).

Eligibility for such benefits may be limited to persons covered by an occupation-based scheme. This is the case in India for the benefits instituted in 1975 by the Self-Employed Women's Association (SEWA), for the maternity grant introduced in the Republic of Korea in 1979 and for the milk coupons issued in Peru beginning in the same year. Nevertheless, the current trend is towards granting such benefits to all residents. This applies in France to the allowances paid before and after confinement, in Luxembourg—since 1974—to pre-natal allowances, in Poland to the grants introduced in 1978, in Finland to the lump-sum grants instituted in 1981, in the United Kingdom to the maternity grant which since 1982 has been paid to all mothers and in Greece, *de facto*, to the grant introduced in 1984.

In many countries such benefits are accorded only if the mother agrees to antenatal and post-natal medical examinations for herself and her child; this usually means that the grants are paid in instalments at the time of each medical check-up, a system which is applied in France. In Luxembourg regular check-ups for pregnant women and infants were introduced in 1977 and are a condition for the receipt of maternity grants. In Austria grants were increased in 1974, provided mother and child attend medical check-ups.

Maternity leave

Maternity leave in the strict sense of the term consists of two components: on the one hand, there is the right of an employed woman to take leave of absence when she gives birth to a child, with the guarantee that she will be able to keep her job, her seniority and her pension entitlement; on the other, there is her right to receive a cash benefit equal to all or part of her previous earnings and payable throughout the duration of her maternity leave.

Since 1975, with only a few exceptions, there has been a lengthening of maternity leave, a loosening up of qualifying conditions—with adjustments to suit individual circumstances—and a broadening of the relevant provisions to cover categories other than female wage earners.

Length of leave

According to a study covering 127 countries, the average duration of maternity leave ranges from 12 to 14 weeks. It lies between these limits in 69 countries, while 31 countries allow shorter leave and the remaining countries a longer period. The shortest periods of leave are usually to be found in the developing countries and the longest in the countries of Eastern Europe. In the industrialised market economy countries there has, since 1975, been a trend towards longer maternity leave.[1] As can be seen, most countries respect the 12-week minimum set out in Conventions Nos. 3 and 103 concerning maternity protection. The following table shows some of the increases in the duration of maternity leave introduced over the past dozen years or so.

Country	Leave
Algeria	From eight to 14 weeks (1974)
Austria	Eight plus eight weeks[1] (1974)
Cuba	From 12 to 18 weeks (1974)
Denmark	Four plus 24 weeks[1] (1985)
Finland	100 working days[2] (1985)
France	From 14 to 16 weeks (1978)
Greece	From 12 to 14 weeks (1984)
Ireland	14 weeks (1981)
Luxembourg	From 12 to 16 weeks
New Zealand	26 weeks[3] (1981)
Norway	From 12 to 18 weeks (1977)
Portugal	30 plus 60 days[1] (1984)
Spain	Six plus eight weeks[1]
USSR	56 plus 56 days[1] (1982)

[1] Pre-natal and post-natal leave. [2] Of which 24 days before confinement. [3] Of which 20 weeks after confinement.

Maternity leave may be of considerable length: 28 weeks in Denmark, five months in Italy (with a further six months of optional leave), 26 weeks in New Zealand, and 26 weeks in Czechoslovakia and the German Democratic Republic.

Tunisia provides a fairly isolated example of the opposite trend, having shortened the duration of maternity leave to 30 days as part of its anti-natalist policy. In a different context, Sweden has reduced maternity leave to 12 weeks but has at the same time introduced parental leave, which can be taken by either the mother or the father.

[1] ILO: *Maternity benefits in the eighties, An ILO global survey (1964–84)* (Geneva, 1985).

The most important exception among the developed nations is the United States where, at federal level, no generally applicable legislative rules exist as regards maternity leave. Only a small proportion of women in certain states or in certain sectors of employment can claim leave, and even then the duration is short—from six to eight weeks in the states which have enacted laws on the subject. It is relevant to note that, despite the recommendations made in 1972 by the Equal Employment Opportunities Commission, the absence of any reference to maternity in private sickness insurance contracts was judged by the United States Supreme Court to be in line with the Constitution.[2]

In most countries a portion of the maternity leave may be taken before confinement. The duration of this pre-natal leave is usually six weeks, but it may be longer—up to 11 weeks in Canada and the United Kingdom. In many cases the minimum amount of leave to be taken before and after confinement is laid down by law, women being free to apportion the remaining leave as they wish. In Austria, Luxembourg, Spain and Switzerland, for instance, it is compulsory to take the whole of the post-natal leave allowance; in Finland, France, Norway and Sweden, a minimum of six weeks must be taken after the confinement; in some countries pre-natal leave is also compulsory, for example in Austria, France and Italy.

In a number of countries longer leave is granted in special circumstances; for the second and subsequent children in Czechoslovakia, the German Democratic Republic and Poland, for multiple births in France, the German Democratic Republic, the Federal Republic of Germany, Hungary, Luxembourg, Poland and the USSR, and for single mothers in Czechoslovakia (up to 12 weeks). The same applies in many countries to difficult pregnancies or complicated deliveries; to give a few examples, up to four weeks additional leave in Ireland (since 1982), four weeks in the United Kingdom and 14 days in the USSR.

Maternity benefits

Together with the lengthening of maternity leave there has been an increase in the sums paid out in maternity benefits, which now tend to depend on the situation of the individual mother. Usually the amounts paid are proportionate to the beneficiary's previous earnings (if necessary a supplementary benefit is added to the standard rate). In most countries the benefit amounts to over 50 per cent of previous earnings, but in industrially developed countries it generally exceeds 80 per cent. In many cases women receive 100 per cent of their previous wages or 90 per cent of net earnings, both in developing countries (for instance in Cameroon, Côte d'Ivoire, the Libyan Arab Jamahiriya, Mali and Senegal, by virtue of measures intro-

[2] General Electric v. Gilbert, Nashville Gas Company v. Satty.

duced in recent years) and in developed countries. Maternity benefits are then higher than the benefits awarded during sickness. In several industrialised countries the proportion is appreciably lower: 60 per cent of earnings in Canada and Japan.

In a number of countries employers are required by law to pay part of the benefit directly as a supplement to the statutory allowances. This is the case in Belgium, the Federal Republic of Germany and Italy. Collective agreements often stipulate supplementary allowances for certain branches of employment or for certain categories of workers.

It is also worth noting that, when maintenance of the woman's full wage is guaranteed, she may well receive a higher net income during maternity leave than when she is working since, generally speaking, maternity benefits are not subject to tax.

Extension of coverage

Originally, maternity leave and maternity benefits were usually granted only to wage-earning women, but now the tendency is to extend these benefits to all women who are obliged to interrupt their occupational activities because of child-bearing. In some countries allowances are also paid to women who do not work outside their own homes, thus providing what is in fact a "maternal wage".

In several countries the number of women entitled to maternity leave and maternity benefits rose to begin with, when social security schemes were extended to activities which were not previously covered, such as work in agriculture, domestic service and self-employment. In Brazil, Ecuador, Jamaica, Mexico, Nicaragua and Venezuela sickness and maternity insurance is now available to domestic staff and to agricultural workers. It was extended to non wage earners in Greece in 1980. In 1983, Gabon broadened the scope of its social security system, maternity benefits in particular (benefits in kind), to cover all nationals. Ireland in 1981 introduced measures protecting all women—wage earners or not—against the cost of bearing children. In 1982 Austria instituted an allowance to be paid to self-employed women for a period of 16 weeks. In France self-employed women have, since 1982, received a lump-sum grant which may be supplemented by an income—replacement allowance.

Certain private schemes are worth mentioning. As noted earlier, in 1975, the SEWA in India introduced a maternity benefits scheme for its members.

In a few countries maternity benefits are paid to all women, including housewives, for a period which may equal that of maternity leave. This is the case in Luxembourg and Sweden. In the latter country parents who have not yet started working have, since 1974, been entitled to benefits throughout the parental leave period, at a guaranteed minimum rate. Parental leave, which has replaced maternity leave, may be as long as 360 days. In Luxembourg the law of 30 April 1980 grants maternity benefits to all women who have been resident in the country for at least one year or whose husband has three years' residence; this allowance is paid for 16 weeks, eight of them before confinement and eight afterwards.

Considering the amounts paid, such benefits closely resemble a "maternal wage". Whether or not they should be granted is the subject of much controversy. By recognising the economic value of women's work in the home, they encourage them to stay there, or at least vindicate this choice as a valid alternative to paid work. This having been said, in the two countries just mentioned most women have an occupation outside their households. In Luxembourg the allowance covers only the period immediately before and after confinement. In Sweden it is part of a policy which aims to reconcile the task of bringing up children with the occupational activities of both parents. The payment of such benefits to women who do not work outside the home then appears less as an innovation than as the outcome of a very broad social protection system as applied to restricted populations—single mothers and persons who have not yet embarked upon their working careers.

Safeguarding jobs during maternity leave

Considerable progress has been made with regard to women's right to keep their jobs when they take time off to have children.

The usual custom is for maternity leave to be accompanied by protection of employed women against dismissal. In France, for instance, women may not be given notice during pregnancy and maternity leave or during the four weeks following the end of the leave period, except in cases of serious misconduct or if it proves impossible to maintain the post (Law of 12 July 1978). In some countries protection goes as far as the right to recover the specific job held before maternity or to be given a similar job. This applies, for example, in Australia, Brazil, Canada (Quebec since 1978), Ireland since 1981 (on condition that the employee has notified her employer of her wish to resume her work with the enterprise), Mexico, the United Kingdom and the United States. In 1978 New Zealand made special provision for cases in which it is impossible to reinstate the woman. In many countries working hours are adjusted to meet the needs of mothers during the post-confinement period (feeding breaks).

Whether or not a woman should be allowed to return to work before the end of her maternity leave is the subject of much debate, which in some countries is reflected in changes in the social security laws.

The desire to protect the health of mother and child has usually led legislators to formulate certain prohibitions or introduce certain obligations which they intend to apply to all women. In such cases, the provisions concerning maternity leave make it compulsory for women to take all or at least part of their leave. This obligation is generally looked on as a safeguard for women, in that it shields them from any pressure to give up their leave, with possible danger to their own health and that of their children.

More recently, a feeling has emerged that this obligation, because it applies to all women, constitutes unjustified discrimination which penalises women's employment: since women are required to stop work for a lengthy period if they have children, employers may be more inclined to take on men. The duration of maternity leave should, therefore, be geared to the health of each individual mother, so as to limit this negative effect. A judgement handed down by the United States Supreme Court illustrates this argument.[3] The Court found that school regulations cannot oblige women teachers to take leave of absence from the end of the fifth month of pregnancy: such a rule assumes that they are incapable of working after the fifth month and interferes with the freedom of choice in family and conjugal matters enshrined in the country's Constitution.

Some countries—the Federal Republic of Germany in 1979 and Austria in the same year—have drawn up their legislations so as to allow women not to take the whole of their maternity leave beyond a certain compulsory minimum. In the Nordic countries in general, even though maternity leave is obligatory, work is not absolutely forbidden and a woman may go back to work before the end of the leave period if a medical examination shows that she is fit to do so. In Denmark the legislation is even more flexible, since there is no obligation to take maternity leave at all. But whereas this arrangement fully respects the working woman's freedom of choice, it obviously has its dangers in that it offers little protection for women vis-à-vis their employers.

The development of maternity protection and the setting of international standards

As a conclusion to this section on the protection of maternity as such, it should be noted that the changes in some legislations have brought up the question of possible revision of ILO standards on the matter, in particular of Convention No. 3 (1919), and Convention No. 103 (1952). In 1975 the International Labour Conference adopted a resolution—the resolution concerning equal status and equal opportunity for women and men in occupation and employment—in which it invited the Governing Body of the ILO to call upon member States to supply reports, with a view to establishing whether the provisions were adequate in the light of the current concept of the right to maternity protection. The Governing Body has examined the question on several occasions. These Conventions are among the instruments to be given priority, but there are no plans to propose further standardisation procedures until another progress report is available towards the end of the implementation period for the 1990-95 Medium-Term Plan.

---

[3] Cohen v. Chesterfield County School Board (21 January 1984).

The ILO standards have come in for criticism on various grounds. Some member States feel that they should be limited to a statement of basic principles and that they are over-specific on such matters as the compulsory nature of post-natal leave, protection of employment during maternity leave, or the spreading of leave before and after confinement. Others feel that the standards have failed to keep pace with certain major developments, such as the extension of coverage to common-law wives and recognition of the father's role in caring for young children.

It would seem that any reconsideration of the Conventions should focus on such matters as the extension of coverage and the nature of the protection provided, whether post-natal leave should or should not be compulsory, the possibility of relaxing the rule forbidding dismissal during maternity leave, qualifying conditions for the receipt of benefits, and the level of allowances and ways of financing them (compulsory insurance or financing from public funds).

The present debate on the possibility of adapting the standards to the changed circumstances is evidence of the concern shown by member States anxious to reconcile women's responsibilities to their own families and those they already assume or now wish to assume in society. Thus, the whole conception of maternity protection has broadened: the important thing is to allow women to enjoy continuity in their working careers and also to acknowledge the role of fathers in bringing up young children. All this has led to the notion of protection for workers with family responsibilities as an extension of maternity protection, through the development of collective child-minding facilities and the introduction of a new entitlement to leave which can be claimed by either one of the parents. These innovations are even more indicative of the progress made with regard to equality of treatment in social legislation than any changes which have occurred in the protection of maternity as such.

PROTECTION OF WORKERS WITH FAMILY RESPONSIBILITIES

The establishment of new standards regarding workers with family responsibilities is the outcome of changes that have taken place over the past ten years in two broad directions. In the first, the aim is to enable both parents to play their part in bringing up the children; in the second, it is to enable women to reconcile their employment activities with their child-rearing responsibilities, in particular by the setting up of collective child-care facilities, thereby promoting genuine equality of opportunity.

These new trends are embodied, internationally, in the Workers with Family Responsibilities Convention, 1981 (No. 156), and the accompanying Recommendation (No. 165) of the same year and, regionally, in the proposed Directive of the European Communities concerning parental leave.

At national level, action has taken two complementary forms: first, the setting up of community facilities (mainly day nurseries), the "collective" organisation of working hours within the enterprise (staggered work schedules) and the development of health and social welfare services; second, the possibility of "à la carte" working hours for individual parents (with parental leave, leave to care for sick children, additional paid leave, and so on). The weight attached to these various types of arrangement has varied between countries, depending on the means at their disposal and their concept of the family and women's role in society.

International standards

ILO standards

Anxious to promote real equality of opportunity and treatment, the International Labour Conference in 1972 adopted a resolution—the resolution concerning women workers—in which it requested the Director-General to work out a coherent programme of activities designed to promote equality, with particular reference to discrimination in training and employment, the guarantee of equal pay for work of equal value and the provision of facilities to enable working parents to meet their family responsibilities. In 1975, in the resolution concerning equal status and equal opportunity for women and men in occupation and employment, the Conference invited the Governing Body of the ILO to place the question of workers with family responsibilities on the agenda for a forthcoming session, with a view to the adoption of a new international instrument. The ensuing debate led in 1981 to the drafting and adoption of Convention No. 156 and Recommendation No. 165, texts which set out new principles and indicated the measures to be taken to ensure their implementation.

The innovative feature of Convention No. 156 is that it recognises that equality in the strictest sense can only apply to workers in identical situations and that the exercise of family responsibilities distorts the position of some workers in relation to others. While the situation of workers in general needs to be improved, special measures will have to be introduced in response to the specific needs of those among them who have family responsibilities.

In a much wider context, the International Labour Conference recognised that the rights of workers with family responsibilities were part of the broader issue of the changing role of the family within society. National policies should take into account the structural changes taking place in modern societies as a result of the changing composition of the family unit and the decline in the marriage rate.

The problem of family responsibilities is recognised in the new standards as one which affects members of both sexes. During the discussions at the

Conference, the Worker members were pleased to note that the problem was no longer seen as an exclusively female issue. The Convention recognises the need to share such responsibilities and that women are no longer alone in assuming the responsibility for family care.

Member States must take all the necessary steps to enable all workers with family responsibilities, male or female, to engage in economic activity without conflict between their family duties and their employment: should the exercise of their family tasks result in temporary absence from work, this should not be a reason for terminating employment.

The establishment of effective equality of opportunity and treatment depends on the adoption of a series of measures that are listed in Recommendation No. 165, which accompanies the Convention. These are designed to enable workers with family responsibilities to exercise their right to vocational training and free choice of employment, to take account of their needs as regards terms and conditions of employment and social security, and to develop child-care and family services. The Recommendation also stresses the need for education and information in the field.

States should make vocational training facilities available to workers with family responsibilities and, where possible, they should be given paid educational leave to enable them to make use of such facilities. They should also make available such services as may be necessary to enable workers to enter or re-enter employment. Family situation should not, as such, constitute a valid reason for refusal or termination of employment.

As concerns conditions of employment, all appropriate measures should be taken to enable workers to reconcile their employment and their family duties, in particular measures designed to improve working conditions and the quality of working life (reduction of hours of work, more flexible working schedules, special arrangements with regard to shift work and night work and the transfer of workers from one locality to another). Part-time and temporary workers should enjoy the same rights as full-time and permanent workers. Either parent should have the possibility of obtaining leave of absence (parental leave) and men and women should be entitled to leave in the case of a child's illness (or that of another member of the immediate family). Similarly, financial assistance—social security benefits, tax relief or other advantages—should be available when necessary. Equal social security treatment should be guaranteed, even during parental leave periods.

Regarding child-care and family services and facilities, the Recommendation invites States to collect statistics on the needs of workers with family responsibilities and to see to it that child-care facilities meet the needs and preferences so revealed. At the same time they should encourage any efforts to reduce the burden of family duties (through family services).

Thus, the new texts define the status of the worker with family responsibilities and indicate the inferences to be drawn. The governments of some developing countries pointed out at the time that the proposed action was perhaps not a priority in countries confronted with the problems of unemployment and underemployment, where the very notion of equality of treatment might conflict with traditional ideas of an opposite nature. Nevertheless, the establishment of minimum standards has the advantage of stimulating national policies—by acknowledging the changes taking place in social structures and focusing attention on the new attitudes they imply—to varying degrees depending on the country. The adoption of the new instruments has led to further action at regional level, in both the European Communities and the Council of Europe.

European standards

Recognition of the rights of workers with family responsibilities has led, in the European Communities, to the drafting of a proposal for a Directive on parental leave and leave for family reasons which was submitted by the Commission to the Council on 24 November 1983.

In the Council of Europe the action taken on resolution 28 (1975) concerning social security for women at home was the subject of a report of the Steering Committee for Social Security dated 15 January 1985. As will be seen, the Council of Europe's approach to the matter is somewhat different.

The European Communities' proposed Directive on parental leave and leave for family reasons, which formed part of the Community Action Programme on the promotion of equal opportunities for women (1982-85), was designed to entitle workers to such leave. The intention was not so much to establish minimum standards or to provide a fixed objective as to harmonise legislations and to remove disparities which could affect the compatible functioning of the Common Market.

The proposed text begins by stating the principle that there shall be no discrimination whatsoever on grounds of sex, whether directly or indirectly by reference, in particular, to marital or family status. This applies to all wage earners, both full time and part time.

In the words of the proposal, parental leave is to be granted to working parents to enable them to stay at home in order to take sole or principal charge of their children. In addition, workers should be entitled to claim a minimum number of days leave per annum for pressing family reasons.

Parental leave should constitute a right and not an obligation. It should be granted to working parents on request, on condition that they give their employers adequate notice of their intention to take leave and to return to work afterwards. The period of parental leave to which workers are entitled should be at least three months, with the possibility of extension for one-parent families or if the child is handicapped. Entitlement to parental leave ceases when the child reaches the age of 2 years, or 5 years in the case of a handicapped or adopted child. Parental leave may be subject to a requirement regarding length of service; it may be taken in part, in which case entitlement to the remaining part ceases. It is to be suspended in the event of the illness of the parent and shall not prejudice any entitlements acquired or in the process of being acquired. Periods of parental leave should be credited in the same manner as periods of maternity leave for the purposes of insurance against sickness, unemployment, invalidity and old age. On termination of leave, the worker should be able to return to the same or an equivalent job.

Regarding leave for family reasons, the proposal lists the following as pressing family reasons: illness of a spouse; death of a near relative; wedding of a child; illness of a child or of the person caring for the child. The duration of the leave may be extended if the beneficiary is head of a single-parent family or has three or more children living at home. For the purposes of remuneration, social security contributions and allowances, and pensions, periods of leave for family reasons should be considered as paid leave.

Incorporation of the Directive into national legal systems, with the consequences this would entail concerning the right of individuals to pursue their claims in the courts, would bring out the full significance of its provisions which, in the European Communities, reflect the international standards with regard to workers with family responsibilities.

Council of Europe resolution 28 (1975) on social security for women at home deals with the matter from a different angle: the aim is not to protect workers who have family responsibilities, but to preserve the rights of women who assume such responsibilities without taking up paid employment. The resolution takes into account the economic activity of women within the home and the time spent, within this activity, in bringing up children. The Steering Committee for Social Security felt that the scope of the text should be broadened and that protection should be provided for all persons who devote their time to household tasks without engaging in outside employment. For the first time, the Committee of Ministers included in its programme of work for 1982 a discussion of equal treatment for men and women in social security.

Action at national level

The principle that workers with family responsibilities should receive social protection has been applied in different ways in different countries, depending on their concept of the role of women in society. States may either opt for collective solutions (by establishing collective facilities for workers and their children, day nurseries in particular, and by promoting health measures and social welfare activities in favour of families) or may help families to care for their children themselves (by allowing parents to interrupt their work temporarily, offering various types of leave of absence and by arranging more flexible work schedules). In practice, financial considerations oblige most countries to choose less clear-cut solutions and to combine the two types of arrangement, the institution of leave compensating for the shortage of collective facilities. In some countries there is, over and above the purely financial aspect, a definite desire to apportion the responsibilities evenly between the family and society as a whole, at the same time leaving individuals some freedom of choice in the matter.

Collective solutions

Collective answers to the problem take various forms, in particular the establishment of community facilities for use by workers and their children and the development of health and social welfare amenities for families.

Community facilities

In an effort to limit the amount of time parents take off from work, some countries have chosen to lower the age at which children start school. Children of pre-school age may attend day nurseries, kindergartens or infant schools; such establishments are particularly common in Eastern Europe.

In Hungary the capacity of day nurseries, which take children under the age of 3, rose from 1,000 places just after the Second World War to almost 47,000 in 1974. Between the ages of 3 and 6, children may attend kindergartens: 83 per cent of the children in this age group did so in 1978. Poland too has made more facilities available. Between 1960 and 1975, the number of children placed in day nurseries (infants under the age of 2) rose from 92,500 to something like 166,000. There has also been a substantial increase in the number of children attending pre-school institutions in the German Democratic Republic. The proportion of children (over the age of 3) enrolled in kindergartens increased from 20 per cent in 1950 to over 87 per cent in 1976. In Czechoslovakia the attendance rates for day nurseries fell between 1960 and 1975; in the latter year 12 per cent of children under the age of 3 were attending them. It should be pointed out that this country was quick to introduce long leave periods for women wishing to look after their children themselves. At the end of 1977 the USSR possessed 120,000 pre-school establishments, which were attended by some 12.6 million children (in 1960 the number was just under 71,000 and the number of children 4.4 million). As can be seen from the foregoing figures, the capacity of institutions catering for small children has increased considerably in all the countries of Eastern Europe, concomitantly with a lowering of the age at which children start school.[4]

---

[4] See ILO: *Work and family life. The role of the social infrastructure in Eastern European countries* (Geneva, 1980).

Collective facilities set up and managed by the State cannot always satisfy the entire need for child-minding. The authorities are often obliged to rely on private facilities which, more often than not, they encourage or even initiate. In principle, any aid provided to such institutions is accompanied by control of the quality of the services they offer, which are usually required to conform to certain standards of comfort and various regulations concerning their operation.

In many countries enterprises employing more than a given number of women are required to provide a crèche. To give just a few examples, this is the case in Argentina, Austria, Bolivia, Chile, India, the Islamic Republic of Iran, Iraq, Italy, Jordan, Myanmar, Romania and the Syrian Arab Republic. In Colombia and Mexico this rule has been replaced by one which requires employers to contribute a uniform amount to the public institutions called on to furnish child-care services.

In the case of facilities set up and managed directly by the State, parents, enterprises and local authorities may be asked to contribute to the cost. Mixed systems also exist, for instance in France (where crèches are financed jointly by parents and the family allowance funds), Hungary and Poland.

At a time when in the developed countries it is no longer possible to provide child care entirely within the family, in the developing countries the breakdown of the extended family is bringing similar problems, and these problems are spreading. In some African countries the organisation of child-minding is left to the population in general, with the authorities providing only subsidiary support. This type of arrangement is to be found in Burkina Faso, Cameroon, the Congo, Côte d'Ivoire and Morocco. Collective facilities may take the form of dispensaries or treatment centres. As part of its Fifth Plan, India has introduced "integrated child-development services" and set up village and local district day nurseries. Thirty-three such projects were put into operation between 1975 and 1978.

Health and social services

In Africa countries such as Benin, Burkina Faso, Cameroon, the Central African Republic, the Congo, Côte d'Ivoire and Senegal, as well as Morocco and Tunisia, have set up health and social welfare services which are mainly addressed to persons with social insurance and members of their families. The emphasis is on protection for mothers and children, pre-school education, informational and educational material and social and medical services.

In other developing countries, in Latin America in particular, social welfare usually covers the whole population, many of whom are not eligible for the cash grants provided by social security. Assistance ranges from help for large families in need—for instance, when the bread-winner has an accident or is otherwise incapacitated—to support services for children and adolescents at all stages of their development: placement of children with foster parents, long-term placement, assistance during school years and when young people start work, and travel and leisure programmes.

In the developed countries, in addition to fighting poverty, health and social welfare activities are more concerned with providing supplementary or family allowances, such as the child-minding allowance in France (this allowance was eventually integrated into family benefits in 1986). Having concentrated mainly on individual aspects of social protection and being already in possession of long-established social welfare services, these countries have not undertaken any major reforms in this field.

Arrangement of working time and leave of absence

Flexible working time

The arrangement of working time to make it easier for workers to fulfil their family obligations has been written into national legislations in a variety of forms. A great deal of progress has been made in this respect over the past few years.

As regards daily work schedules, a continuous working day allows workers to get home earlier. Staggered working hours help them to avoid the inconvenience of having to use public transport during rush hours and make it easier for them to do their shopping and other errands. A variable working day also helps to solve some of the problems of child-minding; for instance, hours can be adjusted to coincide with the opening times of crèches.

Another possibility is a voluntary reduction in the total number of hours worked. Part-time jobs enable workers to engage in paid work while leaving enough time to fulfil family obligations and bring up children. Such modifications have spread considerably over recent years, particularly in the Anglo-Saxon countries, as was seen in the first part of this study.

Leave of absence

Several types of leave of absence have been introduced to make it easier for workers to meet their family responsibilities, for example, leave for the purpose of child-rearing and leave in case of adoption. Leave may be granted to care for a sick child or family member and parents may qualify for additional days of annual leave.

Over the past 20 years, maternity leave has been extended by granting additional leave, paid or unpaid, for the care of infants. Austria instituted such leave in 1961 and Hungary in 1967. Other countries soon followed suit.

The duration of the leave ranges from several weeks to three years, depending on the country. The following table gives some examples.

Country	Leave
Austria	One year[1] (1977)
Canada	24 weeks (1984)
Cuba	Nine months[2]
Czechoslovakia	Up to child's first or second birthday[3]
Finland	158 days (1985)
France	Two years (1977)
German Democratic Republic	Up to child's first birthday
Germany, Federal Republic of	Ten months (1986)
Hungary	Up to child's third birthday
Iceland	Three months (1981)
Ireland	Four weeks (1981)
Italy	Six months
New Zealand	Six months[4]
Norway	One year
Poland	24 months[5]
Spain	Three years
USSR	Up to child's first birthday

[1] For single mothers: three years. [2] Before child's first birthday. [3] According to whether mother is raising one, two or more children. [4] For public employees. [5] Before child's fourth birthday.

Among the countries which have introduced child-care leave are Belgium (for public employees), Egypt, India (for public employees), Israel, Kuwait, the Syrian Arab Republic and Tunisia (for public employees). In several countries, Sweden for example, leave may be split and taken at any time up to the child's third birthday.

There are still many countries where child-care leave is not remunerated. In others, an allowance is paid. In Bulgaria two years' paid leave of absence (extended in 1985) may be followed by a period of unpaid leave up to the child's third birthday. In Finland post-natal leave may be extended from 234 to 300 days and may be followed by six months' unpaid leave. Sweden allows for the possibility of total interruption of employment or of half-time employment until the child is 18 months old, followed by reduced working hours until he or she reaches the age of 8 or is in the first year of school, with payment during 360 days. In the USSR leave is partly remunerated until the child is 1 year old; afterwards unpaid leave is possible up to the age of 2. In some countries the allowances paid are proportionate to wages. Sweden pays 90 per cent of earnings with a guaranteed minimum rate, while in Italy the amount is 30 per cent. Austria and Canada pay unemployment benefit on an income-tested basis. In some countries where only unpaid leave is granted, acquired rights (the right to paid holidays, for example) are guaranteed and social coverage maintained: this applies to Austria and France, and to the USSR as concerns the unpaid leave period.

The common denominator in child-care leave, in so far as it follows on maternity leave, is that it is accompanied by protection of women against dismissal or by provisions facilitating their reinstatement after the interruption of employment. Provisions forbidding dismissal exist in the Eastern European countries, in Austria, Finland, France, Ireland, Norway and Sweden. Beneficiaries are required to give their employers advance notice of their intention to take the leave.

In some countries, though so far they are few, leave may be taken by either the father or the mother and is then known as "parental leave". This is the case in the Scandinavian countries, and in Belgium, Canada, Finland, France and Italy, for example. This formula respects the principle of equal treatment of men and women and encourages the sharing of family tasks between the father and the mother. It may be noted, however, that many more women take advantage of parental leave than men and that they take it for longer periods. In Sweden in 1980, for example, in only 10 per cent of cases was part of the post-natal leave (remunerated by the parental allowance) taken by the father, the proportion rising to 30 per cent for part of the subsequent leave (remunerated by a special parent's cash benefit): these rates were, however, rising. When leave is not remunerated, it would seem that it is mainly the least-skilled, lowest-paid women who make the most use of it, as for example, in Hungary. Independently of how men and women envisage their working careers, it would seem that the level of remuneration plays a major part in the decision as to which parent should take the parental leave.

There is no denying that the introduction of child-care leave has improved the treatment of mothers with family responsibilities in that it enables them to interrupt their work if they so wish while benefiting from certain financial and social guarantees. At the same time, such leave has made it possible in some countries to compensate for the shortage of collective child-minding facilities. Duration of leave, qualifying conditions and payment methods vary widely from country to country and are an excellent indicator of population and social policies in that, quite apart from the desire to improve social well-being, pro-natalist policies and the wish to lower female employment rates (or, on the contrary, to maintain these rates and preserve the role of community facilities as part of the social structure) affect the terms on which leave is granted in individual countries.

From the point of view of equal treatment, the introduction of parental leave (to be taken by either father or mother), improved terms for the granting of allowances, the possibility of taking the leave in several stages and working shorter hours are opening up interesting prospects in several countries. In fact, in some cases the distinction between maternity leave and parental leave has simply disappeared, having given way to a single lengthy period of leave, to be taken at will by either of the parents, during which an allowance is paid. In this way, some States give preference to parental leave over maternity leave, considering that the former is more in keeping with the principle of equal treatment and with modern attitudes to child-rearing.

In Sweden the aim is to enable parents to share their responsibilities and to reconcile their employment with their domestic activities. This policy is based on two major premises. The first is that families need two incomes from employment: consequently, the period of absence from work after the birth of a child should be limited in the interests of all concerned—parents, children and the community. The second is that nothing can take the place of care by the child's own parents. The Government has provided crèches and kindergartens, but at the same time has introduced parental leave and has made it possible for parents to work shorter hours, while paying them allowances which guarantee a certain level of income. This innovative example has so far been followed by only a few countries and to a much more limited degree. Nevertheless, the solution offers considerable advantages in that it provides a balanced response to the problem of child care in modern societies, both as regards social organisation and methods of financing.

In many countries special leave is granted to women or to couples who adopt a child, and adoption may entitle them to social security benefits. In the USSR women who adopt a child at birth are eligible for leave until the child is 56 days old. Denmark has introduced an "adoption grant", payable to the adoptive parents. Israel and Poland have done the same, but the grant is paid to the adoptive mother. In Finland adoption entitles the adoptive parents to an allowance during a minimum of 72 days and a maximum of 162. In 1976 France introduced maternity benefits for adopted children (for a period of eight weeks). Norway has extended payment of maternity benefits equal to full earnings to adoptive parents: in calculating adoption benefits, the legislation takes into account the child's age (under 1 year, between 1 and 5 years).

A new type of leave has been instituted in many countries to allow for the care of children or other family members when they are sick, an event which often creates serious problems for people who work outside the home. The provisions vary considerably as regards the persons who may take the leave, its duration and the terms of its remuneration. Unlike the additional annual leave granted in some countries (see below), leave to care for sick relatives usually entails the payment of social security benefits, either special benefit or sickness benefit.

In respect of care for sick children, the legislation usually fixes an age limit. Leave is granted up to the child's first birthday in Chile, up to the age of 3 years in Italy, 8 years in the Federal Republic of Germany, 10 years in Finland, Hungary, Norway and Portugal, 12 years in Sweden and 14 years in Poland, the German Democratic Republic and the USSR.

The duration of the leave may be expressed in days per illness: three days in Czechoslovakia, seven in the USSR. It may correspond to a given number of days in any one year: 60 days in Poland, two months (for one child) in

Bulgaria, four weeks (for one child) in the German Democratic Republic, six weeks for two children and eight weeks for three or more; it is granted for the whole duration of the illness for children under the age of 12 months in Hungary, with a limit of 60 days for a child between the ages of 1 and 3 and 30 days for a child between the ages of 3 and 10; additional unpaid leave may be requested for the whole duration of the illness when the child is under the age of 10. In the USSR leave is prolonged if the mother is single, widowed or divorced.

Portugal allows 30 days' leave a year and Sweden 60 days per year (for each child).

In the German Democratic Republic leave is granted to single parents and in some countries, Austria, Hungary, Israel, Norway and Sweden, for instance, leave may also be taken by the father.

Leave of absence from work may be granted during the sickness of persons other than children. In Austria leave may be taken to look after any close relative living in the same household. In Sweden either the father or the mother may apply for leave when the person who habitually looks after a child is sick. Lastly, mention should be made of a measure which to some extent resembles the above: in the Federal Republic of Germany the cost of household help is reimbursed when the mother is in hospital and when she returns home if she has a child below the age of 8.

One last measure is deserving of attention: the granting in various countries of additional days of annual leave for family reasons. Very often the legislative provisions in the matter are completed by clauses in collective agreements. Usually only women are entitled to this additional annual leave, but in some countries fathers too are eligible. For instance, in Poland a father bringing up a family alone is entitled to two additional days per year, as is the mother.

The amount of additional leave often varies according to the number of children. In France female employees under the age of 21 are entitled to two extra days per dependent child. In Hungary annual leave for female workers is extended by two days when they have three non-working children under the age of 18: for each child over that number, the mother is entitled to two additional days up to a maximum of 12 days per year (for eight children). Annual leave may also be extended according to the nature of the work or the amount of care required by the children. This is the case in the German Democratic Republic, where longer leave is granted to women workers with three children, to women engaged in shift work with two children and to mothers of seriously handicapped children.

In some African countries—Burkina Faso, Cameroon, Mali—women may take two extra days' leave per child below the age of 15. In Gabon and Guinea this additional leave is accorded to women with children under 14.

Protection of mothers before and after the birth of a child has been greatly expanded and reinforced over the past ten to 15 years. In many countries it has now taken a new turn by covering the period spent in caring for young children.

The desire to enable women to reconcile their family responsibilities with the exercise of an occupation, which has guided many States in their policies, has in certain instances brought about changes which are both innovative and extremely significant from the point of view of equal treatment, in that they permit fathers as well as mothers to take advantage of the new arrangements.

6 FROM THE DEVELOPMENT OF DERIVED RIGHTS TO THE CREATION OF PERSONAL RIGHTS FOR WOMEN

Since 1975 increasing emphasis has been placed on the need for all women to have access to social benefits in their own right. Such individual rights are regarded as a decisive factor in achieving equal treatment for men and women in social security. But before going on to examine the latest developments in national legislations, it is necessary to define the terms of the problem.

PERSONAL RIGHTS AND DERIVED RIGHTS: THE DEBATE

"Personal right" is the term used to describe the right of an individual to social benefits in his or her own name. This right may stem from the person's own occupational activity or from the fact that he or she resides in a given country. It is independent of marital status or family situation, except that in some cases benefits may be increased when there are dependants.

"Derived right" is the right of an individual to receive a social benefit by reason of his or her dependence, real or presumed, on a person who is covered by social insurance. The right usually depends on the individual's marital status, which is often taken as proof of the existence or absence of such dependence.

These two notions correspond to two types of social security scheme: universal schemes and schemes based on occupational activity.

In universal schemes, which are usually funded from taxation, the country's entire resident population, whether gainfully employed or not, is entitled to social security benefits on the same terms. The amount of the benefit does not depend on the amount of income derived from employment. In principle, there is no place for derived rights in a universal scheme.

In schemes based on occupational activity, only the persons exercising such an activity are entitled in their own right to the social benefits in question. These are calculated in relation to earned income and are proportionate to the contributions paid by the insured person. Persons who do not engage in paid employment can in principle benefit only from rights acquired through the contributions paid by an insured person on whom they are dependent.

It is, therefore, in employment-related schemes that the question of personal rights for women arises—in particular for women who do not work outside the home. In fact, this is a problem which concerns all countries, even those in which universal schemes guarantee basic protection for the whole population. In such countries the basic scheme is more often than not supplemented by employment-related schemes funded by contributions, which provide insured persons with benefits proportionate to their previous earnings, thereby bringing their income above the minimum subsistence level.

Given the changes now taking place, whereby the dependent woman is ceasing to be the social norm, the development of personal rights for the female population would appear to be highly desirable. Personal rights would provide a better response than derived rights to the problems of divorced or separated women and unmarried women with family responsibilities, of whom there are so many today: they are a key factor in ensuring equality of treatment for men and women.

The development of such rights appears, however, to depend largely on the development of femalc employment.

In the circumstances prevailing today, when in most countries a large proportion of women are still not in paid employment, the funds available to social security are insufficient to provide non-working women with the same level of protection as that offered to those who do work. It would be difficult to gain acceptance for the transfers of resources necessary to provide such protection, whether they are funded by increased contributions from all contributors or only from the households concerned, or take the form of the sharing of entitlements between men and women.

It would seem, then, that only if a high proportion of women are in gainful employment will it be possible to consider granting them the same entitlements during their periods away from the paid labour force (particularly those occasioned by the presence of children) as those accorded to persons who are in employment. If economic growth is slow, stationary or even negative, it might be necessary to resort to job-sharing between men and women, and sharing of the corresponding income; in other words, there might have to be new work patterns for all concerned.

Recent changes in the situation, especially in the developed countries, are cause for some concern. Far from progressing towards closer integration of women into the working milieu, modern societies more often than not tend to endorse the idea of differentiation and dual standards in social status. For women who are doomed to unemployment or relegated to such forms of activity as part-time or casual work, with no prospects of advancement, any social protection they may be able to acquire in their own right leaves much to be desired.

As regards family structures, the present period is one of transition. Social security, which is still largely patterned on traditional models, provides only a limited response to the transformations now taking place.

THE IMPROVEMENT OF DERIVED RIGHTS

Among derived rights should be included not only the rights acquired by the spouse or other dependants of the insured person, but also the increments accruing to the insured person because of the dependency. Women who are not in paid employment benefit, directly or indirectly, from the two forms of entitlement, both of which are founded on the same principle, namely that women acquire rights only because of their status as dependants.

With more and more women entering the labour force, and a rise in the number of women who are heads of families and of cohabiting couples, schemes which offer derived rights only have provided only a limited, partial response. Rights have been extended, though not yet in all cases, to cover common-law wives and divorced or separated women. Benefits have been improved somewhat, but are limited by the financial resources available and are still—again for financial reasons—subject to fairly restrictive qualifying conditions.

Moreover, derived rights do not cover the whole range of social protection. Whereas in the sickness and maternity branch they entitle dependants to non-cash benefits or certain lump-sum maternity grants, in no country do they provide women with a daily maternity allowance. In the branches dealing with pensions, and occupational accidents and diseases, derived rights do provide dependants with survivors' benefits, in the form either of a lump sum or a pension. In the unemployment branch, on the other hand, the only advantage is that unemployment benefit is increased for persons with dependants.

Coverage still incomplete

The extension of coverage by means of derived rights has taken three forms: the introduction of new derived rights for the spouses of insured persons or the reinforcement of existing rights; broadening of the notion of dependant to include common-law wives; the maintenance of social protection for separated or divorced women after the formal dependency link has been broken.

Introduction of new derived rights for spouses or reinforcement of existing rights

This extension of coverage has been particularly marked over the past ten years in developing countries. In developed countries, over the same period, existing schemes have been reinforced and coverage has been somewhat broadened.

In developing countries the setting up of social security schemes has generally been accompanied by the introduction of benefits in favour of dependent spouses.

Many countries have instituted survivors' benefits for spouses, which usually range from 50 to 70 per cent of the pension (old-age or invalidity) being drawn or which would have been drawn by the insured person. Benefits are usually also awarded to orphans, which may entitle the widow to full survivors' rights when she has children to support; in such cases, the age condition for payment of a survivor's pension is usually waived.

Among the countries which have introduced survivors' benefits or have revised existing benefits are Algeria (1979, for widows of persons drawing invalidity pensions), Burundi (Decree of 16 October 1981), the Central African Republic (Law of 16 April 1981 and Decree of 10 August 1983) and the Libyan Arab Jamahiriya (Law of 14 April 1980); Nicaragua (1983) and Uruguay (Constitutional Decree of 23 October 1979); Malaysia (Law of 25 April 1984) and the Philippines (Decree of 31 May 1977). In Tunisia a new benefit has been instituted within the framework of the general system under a law enacted on 12 February 1981: a death grant equal to one year's wages (with a fixed ceiling), the amount of which is increased by 10 per cent for each dependent child and which is paid to the insured person's beneficiaries. Some countries have extended survivors' rights to unmarried adult daughters who care for their parents: this provision was introduced in Uruguay in 1979. Many countries pay higher old-age or invalidity pensions when the insured person has dependants.

In the sickness branch, derived rights are often limited—as are in fact personal rights—by a shortage of social and health-care infrastructure. Coverage was extended to members of the insured person's family in Guatemala in 1980, in Nicaragua in 1983, in Peru in 1979 and in Turkey in 1981. Similar arrangements exist in Ecuador as part of the rural social insurance scheme covering family members which operates in agricultural communities, co-operatives, associations, committees or other forms of agricultural organisation (Decree of November 1981).

In the family allowances branch, some countries have improved women's social protection by paying benefits of the supplementary family income type. Benefits of this nature increase the family's income; they are also intended, given the extent of unemployment and the lack of employment opportunities, to encourage women to stay at home. Thus, under the Law of 28 May 1980, Tunisia extended to the private sector payment of the "single salary allowance" which was already in force in the public sector: a decree issued on 28 May 1981 broadened this provision to include old-age pensioners and persons drawing invalidity and survivors' pensions. Equal to half of the maximum family allowance (which had been frozen since 1952), this supplement, together with family allowances, in 1981 provided for families with three or more children an income corresponding to 27 per cent of the minimum guaranteed wage for a father with four children.

Over the same period, developed countries were consolidating their existing social security schemes. Basic schemes now cover almost the entire population, with the exception of just a few occupations. Extension and improvement of the schemes covering non-wage employment have in most cases led to reinforced protection for spouses working on family land or in family businesses or to the institution of such protection where it did not exist, mainly by means of derived rights. In countries with a social security system based mainly on a universal scheme covering the whole population (many of the Anglo-Saxon countries, for instance), there is still room for considerable progress in occupational schemes.

In supplementary pension insurance schemes, coverage for dependent spouses has often improved. In the United States, under the Law of 2 September 1974 concerning income maintenance for retired persons, all private pension schemes have since 1979 had to provide for the possibility of extending coverage to the surviving spouses of married employees. Survivors' pensions awarded in this way are not to be lower than half the pension due to the retired person. In Canada private pension schemes have been encouraged to include survivors' pensions among their benefits. In 1978, 44 per cent of persons affiliated to such schemes were members of schemes which pay survivors' benefits, usually equal to half the amount of the benefits due by way of direct entitlement. In the United Kingdom reforms introduced into occupational pension schemes in 1973 and 1975 guarantee the right to a pension of widows of insured persons who die before reaching retirement age; before these reforms, such widows lost most of their entitlement.

Extension of the notion of dependent person to common-law wives

In Western countries cohabitation is in many cases now preferred to marriage. Some social security schemes have adjusted to this new state of affairs by according the benefits of derived rights not only to spouses but also to any person cohabiting with, and financially dependent on, an insured person.

In the sickness branch, extension of the notion of dependent person in most developed countries—European countries in particular—goes hand in hand with recognition of the fact that health care is a basic need and that the whole population, whether economically active or not, should be protected. Medical care is now available to certain persons cohabiting with the insured person who do not qualify for any other social benefits, whether or not they are officially married or related to the insurance holder.

In Belgium a Royal Decree issued on 16 May 1980 granted a derived right to medical care—in the absence of a dependent spouse—to a person of either sex who takes care of an insured man's or woman's household free of charge. This person must have been registered as a member of the household for at least six months; his or her income must not exceed a given amount. In France, by virtue of the Law of 2 January 1978, an insurance holder's common-law spouse who is completely, permanently and genuinely dependent on him or her enjoys a derived right to the benefits in kind provided by the sickness insurance. In some countries, Luxembourg and Uruguay, for example, this right may be granted to a family member other than the spouse, if the person in question looks after the insured person's household.

The definition of dependent person has also been widened in connection with survivors' pensions. Some schemes confer entitlement on individuals who are financially dependent on an insured person and run the household. In Sweden benefits in the occupational injury and pensions branches are awarded to women who, at the time of the insured person's death, find themselves in the same situation as widows; that is, to women who have given birth to or are pregnant with a child of the deceased person or who had lived with him in marriage-like conditions for at least two years. The same applies in Norway, in the same branches, if the woman is maintaining the insured person's children and if she herself was dependent on him, and in Denmark in the occupational injury branch (survivors' pensions in the old-age branch no longer exist in Denmark) if, at the time of the accident or illness, the woman had been cohabiting with the insured person for at least five years. Such benefits also exist in the United Kingdom in the occupational injury branch for women who were living with the victim of the accident and looking after his children, for as long as she maintains them; and in Luxembourg, in the same branch and also in the pensions branch, a family member (a sister or daughter, for instance) who was running the household and was dependent on the insurance-holder's income is also covered.

Maintenance of social protection for divorced or separated women

Under the system of derived rights, it is difficult to maintain adequate ongoing protection for women who are divorced, separated or deserted by their husbands, in that the dependency relationship which linked them to the insured person and which entitled them to benefits has been severed. Efforts have been made to adapt schemes so as to include certain short-term benefits in cases of divorce, separation or desertion and to safeguard the woman's right to a survivor's benefit in the pensions and occupational injury branches on the death of her husband or ex-husband. The arrangements differ from country to country; they are strongly influenced by the provision of family law, which are themselves extremely varied. Social security legislations reflect the changes in such provisions, in particular the disappearance in many countries of the notion of "guilty party" in divorce cases.

We shall first examine the short-term benefits granted in the sickness and family allowances branches and will follow with a review of long-term benefits in the pensions and occupational injury branches.

In occupational schemes family benefits are due to all persons in the given occupation. Most schemes, however, allow the benefit to be paid to the parent who actually cares for the child, even if that parent is not employed. Thus, in the contingencies examined here, family allowances usually continue to be paid to the woman who maintains the child or children, although she herself may not exercise an occupational activity. Solutions differ from scheme to scheme and benefits may be granted on the basis of the ex-husband's insurance, on that of the common-law husband or even on that of another family member. This is true in Czechoslovakia, Hungary and Poland (where, in principle, the woman is assumed to be in paid employment) and also in Belgium, Israel, Italy and Switzerland.

Whereas a desire to protect the children in cases of divorce, separation or desertion usually means that family allowances continue to be paid to whichever parent maintains the children, in schemes based on occupational activity and derived rights, women usually lose their protection against sickness; only rarely is their entitlement maintained.

In Belgium separated spouses keep their status as dependants if they take care of a child or have been awarded alimony. In the Federal Republic of Germany and Spain they are entitled to medical treatment. The same applies in France if there are dependent children. The possibilities are even more limited in case of divorce. In Spain the ex-spouse continues to benefit from medical care; in France this entitlement lasts for one year after the divorce or until the youngest child reaches the age of 3. In most countries where the basic social security schemes are linked to employment, children maintained by the mother continue to benefit from the father's sickness insurance.

In the pensions and occupational injury branches the right of divorced or separated women to survivors' benefits varies considerably and often depends on whether they are receiving alimony.

In Finland, Greece, Ireland, Israel, Japan, Mexico, Romania and the USSR the wife loses all right to a survivor's pension after divorce. In some countries this loss of entitlement is justified by the existence of personal rights for divorced women, for instance in Belgium, Canada and the United Kingdom.

In many countries the wife is entitled to a survivor's pension only if she was receiving alimony. There are two reasons for this qualifying condition. Firstly, the ex-wife who receives alimony depends for her upkeep on her ex-husband's resources: it is only right, therefore, that she should receive the same benefits as a wife who is dependent on her husband. Secondly, in some countries where the award of alimony is still contingent on the absence of guilt, survivors' rights are also linked to this criterion. These principles apply in Austria, Czechoslovakia, Denmark (in occupational schemes), Hungary, Italy, Poland, Switzerland and Yugoslavia.

Lastly, some other countries grant divorced women the advantages of survivors' benefits when they meet the conditions imposed by common law, which are generally linked to age, invalidity or the presence of dependent children; this is simply an application of the logic on which social insurance is based. France, Luxembourg, the Netherlands and the United States fall into this category.

As can be seen, the extension of coverage by means of derived rights has followed various patterns. It has made it possible to reinforce protection for some sections of the working population by improving that of dependent spouses. It also reflects the efforts of occupational social security schemes to adjust to changes in family models—efforts which so far have had only a limited impact, one which varies considerably according to the risks to be covered and the types of situation in which protection is required. While it is fairly easy to imagine that social coverage for common-law wives will become the norm, in that it is merely an adaptation of social security rules to the new mores, maintenance of protection for divorced and separated wives involves major questions of principle—in particular as regards short-term benefits—and leads to fairly serious administrative complications, the problem of how to share the pension entitlements of a deceased person between a surviving spouse and an ex-spouse being a good example.

Limited improvements in benefits, with maintenance of strict qualifying conditions

All attempts to raise the level of cash benefits paid to survivors in the pension or occupational injury branches are limited by the financial capacity of the social security schemes in question. Several factors are involved, the most important being the large number of widows and the fact that they are living longer: any increase in their social security benefits, however modest, implies considerable financial outlay.

Improvements in survivors' pensions may take various forms: a rise in the proportion of the insured person's pension that would be payable (from 50 to 52 per cent in the pensions branch in France, under the terms of the Law of 13 July 1982; from 30 to 35 per cent in the occupational injury branch in Switzerland under the Law of 20: March 1981); variable rates according to the age of the widow (from 50 per cent if the widow is aged under 45 to 70 per cent if she is over 55 in Costa Rica since 1981); prolongation of the benefit period (five years instead of three for widows under the age of 55 in Panama—Law of 23: February 1981); and relaxation of the rules concerning the accumulation of derived entitlements and direct benefits (1979 reform in the United Kingdom).

These fairly modest improvements in derived entitlements have been accompanied by the maintenance of strict qualifying conditions aimed at pinpointing the real needs of survivors. The trend is towards limiting long-term survivors' pensions to those who were financially dependent on the insurance-holder, whose death may leave them in poverty and unable to find new employment and, for the remaining cases, to limit the duration of the benefit. Thus, in most schemes lifelong pensions are awarded only to survivors who have reached a given age, to those who are handicapped or incapable of working, and to those who have dependent children. When these conditions are not met, the duration of the benefit is usually restricted. The increase in female employment implies that a woman who is in good health and has no dependent children should be capable of supporting herself, and the survivor's benefit—usually in the form of a death grant or a temporary widow's benefit—is intended only to cover expenditure connected with the death as such and to tide her over until she can find a job.

The United Kingdom, for example, makes a distinction between the widow's allowance paid to women under the age of 60 during the 26 weeks following the husband's death and other benefits paid to widows who meet certain qualifying conditions or who have children to support. In France the Law of 17: July 1980 introduced an income-tested allowance for widows below the age of 55, of variable duration (three years at most), with the amount decreasing from year to year. Similar arrangements are in force in such dissimilar countries as Czechoslovakia, Nicaragua and Switzerland. In Sweden also, in the pensions branch, a distinction may be made between temporary and lifelong pensions, depending on the survivor's circumstances.

In a few schemes the length-of-marriage condition for survivors' pensions is waived when there is a child of the marriage. This is the case in Austria (in the pensions branch), in Belgium (following the 1984 reform), in France (Law of 13 July 1982) and in several French-speaking African countries. Usually the right to a survivor's pension ceases if the beneficiary remarries, but provisions recently introduced into some legislations allow for resumption of payment if the second marriage is dissolved and has given rise to no entitlement. This is true of most European countries.

In conclusion, it must be admitted that major inequalities exist as regards women who are in receipt of survivors' benefits. Women who have exercised an occupation or who have their own personal incomes may accumulate benefits from their derived rights, from their personal entitlement and from other sources of income, whereas others, especially older women, may have only their survivors' pensions to live on. For these older women, the fact that benefits are indexed neither to the cost of living nor to wages has, in many cases, proved to be a great disadvantage. Often little thought has been given to the benefits accruing from derived rights which, given the current increase in female employment and changing moral values, may mask situations which, in fact, are becoming more and more diverse. Changes are needed if the gap between the over-protected and the under-protected is not to widen still further.

The improvement of benefits stemming from derived rights and extension of these benefits to cover new categories of beneficiaries is a great step forward for non-employed women. This being said, however, the rise in female employment rates has introduced serious imbalances into the existing models of social protection. There would appear to be less and less justification for granting protection derived from the husband's activity to young women who have an occupation, a fact which, for that matter, explains the continuing existence of stringent qualifying conditions for survivors' benefits. Such forms of benefit should be reserved for women who, because of their reduced work capacity or low remuneration, are in genuine need. It would then be possible to provide such women with reasonable pensions without having to spread the available resources too thinly over a large number of beneficiaries. The system of derived rights makes it difficult to ensure the provision of complementary protection and to adapt to new patterns of social behaviour: this difficulty is one reason for the current development of personal rights for women.

THE DEVELOPMENT OF PERSONAL RIGHTS FOR WOMEN

Personal rights for women who are not in paid employment, or who have withdrawn temporarily from the labour market, have developed rapidly over the period under study. Depending on the source of the funds, a distinction can be made between, on the one hand, the free entitlements financed by all the workers contributing to a scheme or by the national community and, on the other, the entitlements financed from the contributions of the women or the households in question. Although this section of the study does not deal with the personal entitlements that employed women may acquire on the same conditions as men, it is worth mentioning as examples of free rights the enhanced entitlements granted to women to offset interruptions of work for family reasons or to compensate for lower incomes.

Free entitlements financed by the community

The institution of free entitlements for women who stay at home reflects, explicitly or implicitly, the value of the tasks they carry out in their households.

Before going further, it would be well to recall some of the theoretical difficulties encountered in determining the value of household activities. Their value can only be assessed in relation to the value of activities in what are mainly female occupations. But the fact that working women more often than not have family responsibilities in addition to their outside jobs often affects the type of work they do and the wages they receive.

There are two ways of calculating the monetary value of household tasks. The first is to determine the cost of corresponding services on the labour market; namely, the amount the family would have to pay to replace the woman in her domestic duties (cleaning women, babysitters, etc.) and the cost of the services (crèches, home helps, mothers' helpers) the community would need to set up to provide equivalent facilities. The second way is to calculate how much the wife could hope to earn if she joined the labour force—in other words, the loss of revenue suffered by the family when a woman stays at home. Whichever method is adopted, in the countries where such calculations have been made the value of household work has been estimated at something like 20-30 per cent of gross national product.

If women who stay at home are to enjoy social protection by virtue of their household tasks comparable to that of women who obtain such protection on the basis of outside occupations, major financial transfers will be required. In the most extreme case, such transfers might possibly lead to the institution of a "housewife's wage", to be financed from taxation or from contributions. In no country does such a wage exist, except perhaps in a rudimentary form in the shape of income-tested family allowances for families with dependent children. There is no example of a "maternal wage" which would provide the housewife with real financial independence. On the other hand, under most social security schemes mothers are entitled, free of charge, to certain benefits designed to compensate for interruptions in their work histories motivated by child-rearing or, more generally speaking, by a need for their presence in the home. Such benefits exist mainly in the sickness, invalidity and old-age branches.

Sickness

In the sickness branch women generally enjoy guaranteed access to medical care during maternity leave and child-care leave. This is the case in the Eastern European countries and in France, for example.

Invalidity

In covering the risk of invalidity, some schemes have broken entirely new ground by making cash benefits available to housewives. New Zealand has played a pioneering role in this respect, with its comprehensive scheme offering compensation for bodily injuries. More recently, in 1981, Israel introduced insurance against the consequences of non-occupational accidents, which covers housewives when they are in hospital, confined to their beds or incapable of carrying out their household tasks. The benefit is funded from social contributions, amounts to 25 per cent of the average wage of insured persons and is paid for 90 days, after a 14-day waiting period. In Finland since 1979 any woman who has to leave employment to care for a small child remains fully protected against the risk of invalidity until the child reaches the age of 3, up to a maximum of nine years (when she cares for three children). Similar benefits exist also in certain non-contributory schemes. For instance, the United Kingdom in 1977 extended invalidity pensions to cover married women who are incapable of carrying out their normal household duties. This benefit, which equals 60 per cent of the standard invalidity pension, is paid for 28 consecutive weeks. In New Zealand income-tested benefits are paid in such situations.

Old age

In the old-age branch a whole series of advantages may be accorded to women free of charge. The relevant provisions are designed to offset gaps in the woman's employment record and, in some cases, to compensate for the lower wages paid to women. These benefits are usually linked either to the husband's or to the wife's income; more rarely, they are independent of both.

In some schemes the old-age pensions paid to divorced women are calculated in relation to thc ex-husband's contributions. In Belgium, for example, half of the sum contributed by him during the marriage is included in the calculation base. In the United States the amount of the pension paid (at the age of 65) to a divorced woman is calculated exclusively according to the ex-husband's contributions, on a 50 per cent basis—as it is for a dependent wife—on condition that the marriage lasted at least ten years (20 years before 1977). In the United Kingdom the size of the pension paid at the age of 60 to a divorced woman who has not remarried is calculated according to the sum of the contributions paid by the ex-husband up to the dissolution of the marriage.

In other cases, the advantages accorded to women free of charge to offset any reduction in their entitlement resulting from the exercise of their household duties are based on their own earnings. The provisions vary from scheme to scheme, but most of them are designed to compensate for periods of inactivity when the pension entitlement is subject to a qualifying period, to credit these periods of opting out as though they were insurance periods or even simply to increase the amount of the woman's benefit, for example according to the number of children raised.

In 1977 the Canadian Parliament voted to introduce into the pension plan an "escape clause" for persons bringing up children (this was to take effect once it had been approved by two-thirds of the provinces): the pension entitlements of the persons concerned were to be maintained in spite of any breaks in employment spent in caring for a child under the age of 7 (this was over and above the maximum allowed at that time for "credited" periods, namely 15 per cent of total working years). This clause was immediately applied in the Quebec pensions programme. In the United Kingdom the years spent at home looking after a child or adult requiring constant attendance have, since 1979, counted towards the number of years required to qualify for an earnings-related pension and are credited for pension calculation purposes. By virtue of the Ordinance of 23 November 1979, the minimum duration of insurance needed to qualify for an old-age pension in the German Democratic Republic is reduced for women by one year for the third child and each additional child; it is also reduced by one year per four-year period during which a woman interrupts her employment to care for a member of her family.

In the basic schemes operating in many countries, non-working periods in the form of paid maternity or child-care leave are credited as insured periods even if the person in question has paid no contributions. Progress in the free crediting of such inactive periods has kept pace with the lengthening of the corresponding leave periods. This is the case, for example, in some Eastern European countries, in France and in Sweden. In Sweden's supplementary pension scheme since 1982 the years during which parents are occupied in caring for children under the age of 3 have been taken into account in calculating pensions. The parents' pension account is credited with one year's income for any interruption lasting for more than six months in any one calendar year. The parental leave introduced in France in 1982 counts as a contribution period for the calculation of old-age pensions.

The free advantages accorded to women may take the form of straightforward increments to benefits. In France's general pension scheme, for instance, the insured period is prolonged by two years for each child raised. It is worth mentioning that many schemes habitually grant women certain advantages with regard to pension entitlement, such as shorter qualifying periods and earlier retirement age. There is no need to go into this subject again; the provisions were fully described and commented on in Part One of the study.

Lastly, it should be pointed out that women are the main beneficiaries of schemes which guarantee a minimum pension. Because their incomes are lower, large numbers of women are to be found among those drawing the smallest pensions, and for them any rise in minimum rates constitutes considerable progress. In France the introduction of a new minimum contributory pension in 1983, with increments according to the number of children, was particularly advantageous to women. Similar provisions have been introduced in the German Democratic Republic, following the 1979 Ordinance.

In the cases we have just mentioned, the free advantages offered to women are based either on the husband's or on the wife's earnings; in other countries, though less frequently, they are independent of both. A good example of this is the old-age pension for mothers introduced in France in 1978. All women with at least three children—or one child under the age of 3—to support and who receive family supplements automatically become members of the old-age insurance scheme. Their contributions are paid by the National Family Allowances Fund on the basis of the guaranteed minimum wage (SMIC) and they are entitled to benefits based on the same guaranteed minimum.

The development of free entitlements, financed collectively by all workers paying social security contributions, for women who are not wage earners or who have had to interrupt their employment is hampered by the financial limitations of the schemes in question, as is the development of derived entitlements. As we have seen, the provisions adopted in such cases are of various types. They may be designed to offset any gaps in insurance resulting from the exercise of family responsibilities, but may also be intended to compensate for the lower level of women's remuneration (the introduction of minimum pension rates or pension increments when there are children). In some countries they may be limited to the crediting of brief periods of interruption of employment (maternity leave, for instance), but in others may guarantee the right to a pension of women who have never worked outside the home (invalidity pensions for housewives, old-age insurance for mothers).

In the long run, the high cost of such measures should lead to more rational methods of achieving progress and to a more precise definition of the situations to be catered for: brief interruptions of employment or permanent economic inactivity. Systematic efforts should also be made to ensure that advantages do not overlap with each other (free credit for periods of inactivity on the one hand and increased allowances on the other) and that together they form a coherent whole.

Contrary as they are to the principle of equal treatment, the provisions under consideration here also raise the problem of fairness to women workers who do not interrupt their employment to bring up their children—women who contribute to social security funds and who assume their family responsibilities without the benefit of most of the advantages offered to women who stay at home. Such a situation is no doubt inevitable during the present period of transition, when the female population is made up of both women who are not in employment at all and others whose employment history is comparable to that of men. One remedy is to pay child-care allowances or to provide free day nurseries.

In view of all these difficulties, some schemes prefer to institute contributory personal rights financed by the women or the households concerned.

Paid entitlements financed by the women or the households concerned

By asking non-employed women or women who temporarily give up their employment to finance their own entitlements (or by asking their husbands to do so), it is possible to avoid giving them an advantage over women who are economically active. It has been observed that, in the countries where steps have been taken in that direction, many households were already making a considerable financial effort to ensure the dependent wife's economic security by subscribing to private insurance schemes, quite apart from social security as such. There was, therefore, nothing shocking in the fact that social security should offer similar protection in return for the payment of cash contributions. But although this reasoning may be valid in the case of fairly well-off households, for others the financial burden may be impossible to bear.

The creation of personal rights for women on a contributory basis has so far moved in two broad directions; one being voluntary insurance and the other the sharing of entitlements between husband and wife.

Voluntary insurance

Many systems offer the possibility of voluntary insurance, in return for the payment of contributions, to mothers who have never worked outside the home or—and this is more frequent—to women to interrupt their work to bring up children, thus enabling them to maintain their social protection. This option exists in the old-age branch in France (since 1975), in the Federal Republic of Germany, Israel, Japan (since 1975) and Luxembourg (since 1974, for craftworkers, small-scale entrepreneurs and merchants). In the sickness branch some examples are the ongoing medical insurance schemes in Belgium, the Federal Republic of Germany and Luxembourg, or the personal insurance instituted in France in 1980 for women with children.

Because of its high cost, voluntary insurance has had only limited success, especially in the old-age branch where the date at which the risk becomes reality is still far off. In Japan, however, following a vigorous information campaign, the number of voluntarily insured persons has risen rapidly: 4 million in 1975, 5.6 million in 1976 and 6 million in 1977.

The contributions may be paid by social assistance services or out of family allowance funds. This is the case in France where, however, this provision covers only the very neediest of women, who have to pass a strict income test.

The sharing of entitlements

The second way of providing contribution-based personal rights for women is for entitlements to be shared. Two examples of this method are to be found: in the Federal Republic of Germany, where the sharing of pension entitlements was introduced in 1977 in cases of divorce, and in Canada, where a similar scheme was adopted in 1978.

In Canada the new provisions of the pension plan and the old-age protection programme which came into force on 1 January 1978 stipulate, in case of divorce or annulment of the marriage, that the pensionable earnings accruing to the spouses during the course of the marriage and recorded in their old-age insurance account be divided equally between them. This sharing of entitlements may take place at the request of either spouse within three years of the dissolution of the marriage, the only condition being that during the course of the marriage they had lived together for at least three consecutive years.

The scheme introduced in the Federal Republic of Germany with effect from 1 July 1977 is even broader in scope. The total pension entitlements acquired by the husband and wife during the marriage, not only in the statutory pension insurance scheme but also in the schemes for public servants and the self-employed, in occupational or enterprise schemes and in schemes operated by private insurance companies, are shared equally between them. In the statutory pension insurance scheme the sharing of entitlements, which takes place at the time of the divorce, confers identical rights on each of the spouses (excluding any entitlement acquired before the marriage). In fact, because of the many different schemes in operation, various methods are used: straightforward sharing of the entitlements, transfer of contributions or the constitution of a separate pension.

In the Federal Republic of Germany, as in Canada, this sharing of pension rights provides the woman either with a personal pension which is independent of that of her ex-husband, or with an increment to any pension rights she may have earned as a result of her own paid activity. These arrangements automatically lead to a reduction in the husband's entitlement. In the Federal Republic of Germany men may if they so wish pay voluntary contributions to make up for the loss suffered at the time of the share-out. If they do not take up this option, a general decline in benefits is to be feared, unless this is alleviated by the introduction of a minimum pension.

There is, however, another danger: that the sharing of pension entitlements in this way could discourage couples from marrying. It is no doubt for this reason that in the Federal Republic of Germany the spouses may choose to opt out of the scheme by signing a contract to that effect at the time of marriage. This system, which helps to ensure equality for men and women within the marriage, in fact does nothing to reduce the inequalities which remain the norm in society as a whole; it has done little to counter the fact that household tasks still go unpaid or that women still play only a minor role in the production process.

The chances that personal rights for women will be extended on a paying basis—that is, personal entitlements financed out of contributions paid by the women or families in question—appear to be slight. This solution does, however, present some advantages in that it is strictly limited to the protection of women who are economically inactive, whereas in fact more and more women are taking up paid employment.

The scope for improving women's social security rights, either derived rights or personal rights which are additional to any entitlements they may acquire through their employment, is today circumscribed by the financial difficulties facing most social security schemes. Only when women are fully integrated into the world of work will they receive adequate personal rights. With genuine sharing of tasks and roles in society, compensation for the periods when women's employment is interrupted for maternity and child-rearing would pose no more of a problem than the crediting of military service periods for men. It might then be possible to leave the responsibility for social protection of men or women whose inactivity is not motivated by the presence of children to the households concerned.

7 WOMEN IN PRECARIOUS SITUATIONS AND IN POVERTY

Over the past ten years the situation of many women has deteriorated.

The agricultural, handicraft and trading activities, which appeared to be a natural outlet for women at home, have declined almost everywhere. Moreover, women's integration into the paid labour force has more often than not occurred in sectors or occupations which are only poorly protected. Women have also been badly hit by unemployment. The only positive trend in female employment has been in the public sector, which has engaged large numbers of women, particularly in health and social services and in education. For this reason, the decline in the number of such posts which has taken place in some countries as a result of the economic recession is giving rise to considerable concern for the future of women.

Precisely because of their financial vulnerability, women suffer more than men from the erosion of traditional family structures. The isolation of unmarried and divorced mothers is responsible for situations of particularly tragic and, alas, all too frequent poverty. In many countries the situation of these women is causing even greater concern than that of older women who, because of widowhood, find themselves facing serious financial hardship.

A PRIORITY: ACTION IN FAVOUR OF WOMEN WITH FAMILY RESPONSIBILITIES WHO ARE IN DANGER OF POVERTY

The difficulties encountered by women with dependent families, which have been aggravated by the current economic depression and the rise in unemployment rates, have found a first broad remedy in the benefits awarded to the neediest families. In addition, specific measures have been introduced to counter a new problem, that of the one-parent family whose head is, nine times out of ten, a woman. Lastly, some States have decided to tackle the problem at the source, preferring vocational training programmes and other measures designed to encourage women to join the labour force to direct financial transfers or social assistance.

Benefits for the neediest families

The concept of social protection has today been broadened to include such contingencies as the renting or purchase of housing, long-term unemployment and divorce. Efforts are being made to co-ordinate employment, social security, social assistance and fiscal policies, and growing importance is being attached to social transfers as a way of raising the incomes of the neediest families. These developments have made it possible to take a wider view of the situation of the poorest families and to offer them more effective help.

There has been some degree of harmonisation of social security arrangements, on the one hand, and social assistance and welfare measures, on the other. On the social security side, the introduction in the family allowances branch of special-purpose income-tested benefits, together with certain fiscal measures, has made it possible to diversify the help provided, while concentrating on the neediest families. On the social assistance and welfare side, an increase in the amount and variety of benefits and relaxation of the qualifying conditions have made it possible to offer more help to those in the greatest need, with guarantees similar to those applying to social security benefits.

More redistributive social security benefits

In the social security field, the fight against poverty, which has been made easier by an overall increase in the level of benefits, calls, as far as women are concerned, for improvements in unemployment insurance and family benefits (quite apart from the question of paid maternal or parental leave, which was raised earlier in the study).

As regards unemployment benefits, no particular progress has been observed. Women, who are more frequently the victims of unemployment than men, have benefited in a general way from the all-round increases. In insurance-based schemes, however, they have been less fortunate, their difficulty in finding a new job reducing their capacity to pay insurance contributions. Some effort has nevertheless been made to give single mothers easier access to vocational training, as will be seen later.

In family benefit schemes, on the other hand, a number of countries have improved matters by adopting a principle of income redistribution whose application is of particular benefit to the poorest families, especially to single mothers.

Income-tested benefits awarded for special purposes play an important part in such schemes. In 1983 the International Social Security Association

(ISSA) carried out a survey of the situation in 22 countries. Almost half of the countries in question had instituted, in addition to benefits which are independent of the family's income level, allowances based on earnings. In all cases, low-income families are the main beneficiaries, receiving either a guaranteed family income supplement (as in France) or increments to basic family allowances (Italy and Poland). In about one-quarter of the countries consulted, the system consists solely of benefits that depend on the level of family income. In something like three-quarters of them, the family benefits branch administers specific kinds of assistance to supplement the basic allowances: orphans' allowances, allowances for the disabled, single-parent allowances and housing grants. These allowances help mainly the categories of the population who are in the greatest need. In some countries, France and Sweden among others, they have done much to keep needy families out of debt.

Efforts have also been made to co-ordinate public policies: this is especially striking in the field of taxation. In traditional systems only the family situation counts in the decision to award family allowances and in calculating their amounts. These allowances are usually not taxed. Some countries also grant tax rebates pro rata to income or, in France, tax relief according to the number of dependants. The combining of these diverse rules results in a system which is in the best of cases neutral in relation to income and in most cases "anti-redistributive", that is, more advantageous to the well-off than to the needy. Some countries have decided to do away with tax relief linked to family situation and at the same time to raise family allowances and make some benefits taxable.

In the Federal Republic of Germany tax relief for families with children was abolished in 1975 and family allowances, which are not taxable, were raised to compensate for the loss. In the same year Israel introduced a single system of non-taxable family benefits to replace the three previous schemes that had given the right to tax deductions. A similar reform took place in the Netherlands in 1976 and in Austria and the United Kingdom in 1977. In the Netherlands the increase in family allowances was weighted according to income, which was not the case in the Federal Republic of Germany, for example.

Taken together, these efforts at redistribution have generally made it possible to provide the neediest families with an acceptable social minimum, despite the ill-effects of the economic crisis. Efforts have also been made to reduce the hardships suffered by needy families by providing more emergency help (for instance, when rent is in arrears) and introducing new payment procedures so as to provide more regular payments and more continuity in their effect.

There are, however, limits to what can be achieved by such methods. Family allowances are still usually tax free. Educated families of some social standing continue to enjoy easier access to collective services. A desire to raise birth rates in the industrialised countries had led to a toning down of the selective character of family benefits linked to income. Lastly, the financial difficulties encountered in managing social security funds have given rise to restrictions which will seriously affect the neediest members of society.

Social assistance and social welfare services: Broader coverage

Continuing poverty has led to the development of various forms of social aid and social welfare activities, either alongside or in place of social security benefits. Qualifying conditions have often been relaxed and social assistance is now provided on much the same basis as social security benefits. This is true both in countries with well-developed social security programmes and in those where various forms of social aid constitute the main instrument of protection.

In Canada, for instance, women with dependent children are entitled to long-term assistance without being required to seek employment. Similarly, in New Zealand a "domestic purpose benefit" has since 1973 provided a minimum guaranteed income to fathers or mothers with children to maintain, and to single women whose resources are below a certain level.

The reforms carried out in Israel and the United Kingdom are also of major significance.

In the United Kingdom the discretionary system applied by the Supplementary Benefits Commission was in 1980 replaced by a system of income-related benefits awarded according to rules laid down by law, with publication of the relevant provisions. Rates depend on marital status and the number of children. The scheme is administered by the Benefit Office of the Department of Health and Social Security.

In 1982 Israel introduced a guaranteed minimum income for all residents, with four types of assistance administered by the National Insurance Institute: supplementary cash benefits linked to the size of the family; free health insurance; rent subsidies; payment of national insurance contributions. At the same time, the income ceiling for receipt of non-contributory assistance was lowered.

In the United States, on the other hand, more stringent qualifying conditions for assistance were introduced in the early eighties both for Aid to Families with Dependent Children and for free medical care. The first of these is granted to families in which one parent is deceased, absent or invalid, and the second follows almost automatically. The restrictions affect women in particular: in 1979, 2.9 million single women with dependent families took advantage of the programmes, making them the largest group by far to receive such aid. Since 1982 the funds available for assistance have been reduced, the rule which allowed beneficiaries to earn small amounts on the side with no reduction in the amount of the grant has been revoked and income testing has become more severe.

As with social security, an effort has been made to co-ordinate assistance measures and tax regulations so as to give most help to the neediest groups. In Australia tax rebates and deductions for children were abolished in 1976, but with a corresponding increase in non-contributory family benefits. In 1979 Canada instituted tax credits for children of families who do not pay income tax (at that time, the amount was Can$200 annually per child for families with incomes of less than Can$18,000). Also in 1979 the United States introduced tax credits on earned income for families with dependent children when that income was less than US$10,000, and a refundable tax credit (maximum US$500) for families with incomes below taxable level.

As regards social welfare services, these have developed most rapidly in developing countries, where they cover the poorest families, either in parallel with family benefits schemes which cover only wage earners—as in French-speaking Africa—or as a supplement to social security—as in Latin America. Benefits in kind, help in cases of extreme distress (danger of the family breaking up in Argentina, for example), educational programmes for women—all these activities aim to provide a global response to the problems of poverty and, more generally speaking, of economic development. They are sometimes accompanied, especially in Asian countries, by the promotion of family planning.

Social security, social assistance and social welfare have, as this section of the study has shown, followed converging paths in providing help for the needy family with numerous children whose head is, more and more frequently, a woman. The aim is, on the one hand, to concentrate aid on the neediest sections of the population and, on the other, to consider the state of poverty in all its aspects. This effort has, unfortunately, been considerably hampered since the early eighties by the constraints imposed by the economic recession. As unemployment rises, poverty is spreading, affecting some population groups for the first time; at the same time, the resources available to finance social protection are dwindling. Social assistance and social welfare services are very often the first to suffer from this state of affairs.

A new problem for social protection: The one-parent family

A study carried out in 1982 in eight countries produced the data given in the table on page 103 concerning single-parent families, families headed by women and lone mothers in the labour force. As the table shows, the single parent is no longer the exception to the rule.[1]

---

[1] Sheila B. Kamerman and Alfred J. Kahn: "Income transfers, work and the economic well-being of families with children: A comparative study", in *International Social Security Review* (Geneva, ISSA), 1982, No. 3, pp. 345-382.

In addition to benefits for the neediest families, whose recipients often happen to be single parents, special measures have been adopted in many countries in favour of one-parent families. These include increments to, or extensions of, common-law provisions, the introduction of specific benefits for such families and arrangements for the recovery of unpaid alimony. But in spite of these efforts, the treatment meted out to single-parent families still varies widely from country to country.

Increments to, or extensions of, common-law provisions

The provisions whereby increments to, or extension of, benefits are accorded to single parents are usually those which concern family allowances, maternity leave and parental leave. In some countries special advantages are also granted with regard to unemployment insurance.

Family allowances are increased for single mothers in Denmark, Hungary, Norway, the United Kingdom and the USSR. In 1981 France lowered the income ceiling for entitlement to means-tested family benefits.

Maternity leave is often extended for single mothers, as is the leave granted for the care of sick children in countries where this benefit exists.

In the Federal Republic of Germany single mothers keep their entitlement to unemployment insurance if they have worked during the preceding year. Still in the domain of unemployment insurance, but in Austria this time, single mothers with a dependent child who have taken their quota of unpaid leave (up to one year from the birth of the child) receive income-tested emergency assistance at the end of that period up to the child's third birthday.

Specific benefits for single parents

Maintenance grants or other specific forms of aid have been introduced for single parents. These benefits are usually distinct from the traditional forms of derived benefit and are granted either in specific cases of isolation—widows, for example—or in all cases of isolation—widows, divorcees and sole parents. These allowances are often accompanied by free health insurance.

The first such benefits to be instituted were the temporary allowances awarded to widows who have not yet reached the age at which they can claim a survivor's pension. These allowances are usually conditional on having a child to maintain or to care for. A good example is the surviving spouse's insurance scheme introduced in France in 1981, which we shall refer to again later. Another case worth mentioning is the temporary allowance paid for one year following the death of the spouse in Hungary.

Single-parent families, families headed by women and lone mothers in the labour force, various countries, 1982

Country	Single-parent families as % of all families	Families headed by women as % of all families	% of lone mothers in labour force
Australia	12.7	10.8	43
Canada	12.3[1]	10.6	63
France	13.0	13.0	69
Germany, Federal Republic of	11.0	9.0	63
Israel	4.3	4.0	69
Sweden	27.0	24.4	86
United Kingdom	12.0	10.4	49
United States	19.5	17.5	68

[1] Families whose head is under 65.

Source: Sheila B. Kamerman and Alfred J. Kahn: "Income transfers, work and the economic well-being of families with children: A comparative study", in *International Social Security Review* (Geneva, ISSA), 1982, No. 3, table 9, p. 368.

In addition, some benefits of wider scope have been introduced.

In Sweden protection for single parents is provided through a combination of subsistence allowances, which are unrelated to income, and of housing grants, which are income-tested and often quite high. These benefits provide single parents with an income equal to the net income of the "average worker".

In France housing grants and income-tested family benefits (orphan's allowance, young child allowance and family supplement) are essential components of the aid allocated to one-parent families. It is also worth noting that the scope of orphan's allowances has been broadened: they are now awarded not only on the death of a parent, but also in cases of divorce or separation. A single-parent allowance was added to these other benefits in 1976. This is income tested and is paid for one year or until the youngest child reaches the age of 3: the result is that the parent receives a subsistence income more or less equivalent to the minimum guaranteed wage, adjusted according to the number of dependent children.

In the USSR single mothers receive a monthly allowance: in 1983 this was 20 roubles per child under the age of 16.

Methods of recovering maintenance payments

In many countries legislators have abandoned the attitude, traditionally embodied in civil law, that the recovery of maintenance payments (alimony and child support) for divorced, separated and deserted women is a private matter. Social security and social assistance services are more and more frequently called on to help women left destitute by the non-payment of the maintenance due to them. To offset their expenditure on such cases they intervene on behalf of the women to recover the debt.

In several countries women may be granted subsidies or advances against unpaid maintenance. This is the case in Denmark, France since 1981 (through family allowance funds), Hungary, Norway and Poland (through the fund set up for that purpose by the Social Insurance Institute) and Sweden. In Sweden, moreover, children continue to receive their maintenance allowance on the death of the debtor, through the basic pension scheme. Arrangements of this nature are as a rule made through public or social security institutions, the body advancing the allowance entering into the rights of the creditor.

Since social assistance services are also more and more frequently called on to intervene in cases of non-payment of maintenance, they have been given the right of redress. In the United Kingdom if a person to whom maintenance is owed receives help from the supplementary benefits scheme, steps may be taken to transfer the debt claim to the body providing the assistance, which will then pay an allowance whether or not the debt is repaid. In Canada, in all but two provinces, the amount of maintenance paid by the husband is deducted from any benefits paid by a social assistance institution, which then has the right to sue for recovery of the debt in case of non-payment. In New Zealand compulsory deductions from wages were started in 1981 to help to support children in families receiving a domestic purpose benefit from social assistance funds.

In all these examples the objective is the same: to help families who are in difficult circumstances by substituting collective responsibility for that of the defaulter. In Poland more than half of the maintenance fund is obtained from state subsidies. Efforts are under way to improve the collection of such debts in order to bring about a corresponding reduction in public expenditure. In some Canadian provinces a "family court" supervises the execution of all judgements involving maintenance payments, without any need for intervention by the wife or the assistance authorities. This action is accompanied by parental support measures.

Vocational training policies and employment opportunities

Improved social benefits make it possible to ensure that women with families who are threatened with poverty receive an income. Nevertheless, the surest and most satisfying guarantee is still the exercise of an occupation which procures adequate remuneration.

There is often a feeling that a sort of compensating mechanism operates on behalf of the neediest women: precarious employment in poorly protected sectors or activities—which makes them more liable to unemployment than men—being offset by more generous assistance; these benefits in turn make their uncertain position in the labour market both possible and more tolerable. This compensating mechanism is now threatened by the financial constraints which of recent years have considerably handicapped social assistance schemes. Much praise is, therefore, due to those countries which have recently made an effort to provide adequate vocational training and new employment opportunities for the women in question.

These efforts are of two kinds: the organisation of vocational training programmes for certain groups of women in precarious situations, and the introduction of certain conditions for the award of benefits which are designed to encourage the beneficiaries to take up employment.

For a number of years now, most countries have, in conformity with the principle of equal treatment, made efforts to improve the vocational skills of women and, in some cases, to encourage them to enter occupations or sectors previously open only to men. Alongside these broad measures, which are not really of direct concern to social security, several countries have taken specific steps to help some categories of women who find it more difficult than others to obtain access to employment; these are usually first-time jobseekers and women who have left the labour force temporarily to bring up their children. These measures, which are an extension of those designed to safeguard jobs during maternity or parental leave but go much further, are often linked to the insurance or social assistance benefits, unemployment benefit in particular, to which women may be entitled from other sources.

In the United States, where previously individual states usually ran vocational training courses for beneficiaries of assistance to families with dependent children, a stiffening of the qualifying conditions has been accompanied by provisions making payment of assistance benefits contingent on the performance of work for the community services which fund them. It is to be feared that such obligations may deter those concerned from taking up normal employment.

On the other side, it is worth mentioning the success obtained in the Scandinavian countries, Sweden in particular, in the battle against unemployment—especially female unemployment. Sweden's policies are based on two premises: the need to safeguard jobs by preventing dismissals and lay-offs, with special measures in favour of women; and the need for special help for mothers in search of their first job and mothers taking up work again after raising their children. The introduction in 1976 of a vocational training allowance independent of the spouse's earnings, together with action by the employment agencies and programmes of work "of public utility", have helped to stabilise female unemployment at a level comparable to that of men. About half the beneficiaries of these programmes are women.

In France steps are being taken in the same direction, although with less tangible results. Starting in 1978, on-the-job training contracts, with no age restrictions, have been offered to single mothers with at least one dependent child, to women who receive the single parent's allowance and to women seeking to return to work within a period of two to five years after the birth or adoption of a child. In such cases the State offers help with adaptation to a given post, as well as with the acquisition of a new skill.

In addition to these measures in favour of vocational training, provisions designed to encourage women to enter the labour force have been introduced into the methods of paying certain benefits. One example is the surviving spouse's insurance instituted in France in 1981: an income-tested allowance is paid to the widow or widower for three years at most, the amount decreasing from year to year, in an attempt to persuade beneficiaries to seek a job. However, unless measures of this type are accompanied by energetic training and placement policies, their effect is merely restrictive.

These few examples, which are given as illustrations only, are evidence of a new and promising attitude to the problem; namely, that one should strike at the root causes of poverty—unemployment or difficulty in gaining access to the labour market—rather than merely trying to offset their effects by means of financial assistance. This approach appears to varying degrees and in various forms in many social security systems, and even more frequently in social assistance programmes. But a close watch will need to be kept on the outcome of such policies, which must not be used to justify a reduction in the amount of assistance provided for the neediest members of society.

As this section of the study has shown, both social security and social assistance have been working to find remedies for the rising poverty rates among women, by shifting the focus to the neediest among them and by adopting specific measures in favour of single mothers. Nevertheless, it would seem that only by integrating women fully into the world of work on terms similar to those enjoyed by men can the current trend towards their exclusion and marginalisation be halted, and with it the ever-growing expenditure on aid and social assistance this entails.

Further action in favour of older women

Elderly women are the main beneficiaries of non-contributory old-age pensions. On the one hand, because of the difficulties they experience in finding a job and the low wages they earn if they do find one, many have only very small entitlements under old-age insurance schemes. On the other hand, because they live longer than men, they are more likely to receive such benefits and to draw them for longer periods. For the same reason, they are more likely to suffer a loss of income in real terms as the value of money declines. Thus it is mainly the female population which has benefited from the improvement in non-contributory old-age benefits which has taken place in most countries over the past few years, either through the development of universal pension schemes or through the introduction of a means-tested guaranteed minimum income, or again through the institution of special allowances for the neediest old people.

Universal pensions are usually financed from taxes and paid in standard amounts to all residents, with different rates for couples and for single persons. They offer an effective, but costly, solution to the problem of poverty among older women without, in some cases, providing more than a mere subsistence-level income. In the countries where they exist—the Nordic countries, New Zealand (since 1977-78) and the Netherlands, for example—they reflect a desire to reduce the inequalities which result from differences in career structures at the moment of retirement.

Most countries prefer more restrictive compensating mechanisms, adopting for instance the formula of a means-tested "minimum social income", which limits the cost of protection. This is usually applied on a nation-wide scale since, in principle, it is based on the overall situation of all the persons concerned, and is a way of supplementing the income derived from old-age pension insurance.

While the improvements in these benefits over the past ten years or so have enabled a number of industrialised countries to raise the income of elderly couples above the poverty line or minimum subsistence level, there is still a long way to go—and this is true almost everywhere—before the situation of elderly single persons, most of whom are women, is as satisfactory. Given the resources available, it is not possible to make full allowance for the fact that the expenses of a single person are not merely half those of a couple: some items cost just as much for one person as for two (housing, heating, etc.). However, efforts to compensate for this have been made in some countries.

In Canada, for example, single persons have since 1979 received special supplements to bring them above the poverty line. The income-tested survivor's pension is maintained for widows up to the age at which they are entitled to a pension in their own right (65). In France the minimum rates of old-age benefit for single persons and couples were brought more into line in 1982, unfortunately in a climate of austerity. In the United Kingdom non-contributory benefits have been introduced for persons over the age of 80 who are not eligible for a normal retirement pension, women beneficiaries being in the majority.

In the future, improvements in the pensions accruing to women as a result of their own employment activities should reduce the importance of these compensatory measures, of which, for the time being, they are the main beneficiaries. In the meantime, it would appear indispensable to pursue the action in favour of women living alone. It is not inconceivable that this will lead to greater solidarity among retired persons themselves, such as already exists between those who are retired and those who are still in employment. In the countries in question pensions tend to carry over into retirement the inequalities of working life, which are then added to inequalities in capital assets, the latter being particularly in evidence among older people. Thus it would appear only natural—although this is not the case at present—to ask retired people to show the same spirit of solidarity as the rest of the population, through taxation and social contributions.

The introduction of special-purpose benefits in some countries has brought considerable improvement in the living standards of the neediest old people. This applies to the housing allowances paid in France (the "social" rent allowance, which raises the income of a single person drawing the minimum old-age pension by about one-third) and in Sweden since 1978. It is also the case for constant attendance allowances, which are sometimes means-tested and which exist, for example, in France and in the United Kingdom, where they were introduced in the 1980s to help cover the cost of care provided by a person who is not a member of the family.

In addition to national benefits of this type, there are the benefits granted by local authorities, in cash or in kind, which are of considerable help to this section of the population, but whose real impact is usually difficult to assess. The fact of receiving non-contributory benefits sets in motion a whole series of services and tax exemptions which lie outside the purview of social security.

And so, in various ways, the position of older women has improved in recent years. But for the oldest among them, and those who live alone, there is still cause for considerable concern. Operation of the financial transfers needed to ensure that they receive the minimum for a decent standard of living calls for a national movement of solidarity to which older people who are more comfortably off will need to contribute.

The "feminisation" of poverty which has been taking place over the past 15 years or so is evidence of the difficulties of social integration for many women who are vulnerable because of their age, family situation or marital status. Confronted with this problem, social protection systems have made a considerable effort to adjust to the situation, in particular through measures in favour of older women, along with more sporadic measures designed to help single mothers. This action must be pursued, if only to offset the disastrous effect that the current economic crisis entails for many women. Even though, indirectly, such measures may infringe the principle of equal treatment for men and women, in that they appear to favour the latter, they will remain necessary as long as specifically female forms of poverty continue to exist. Ultimately, however, the real response to the difficulties engendered by the precarious financial situation in which many women find themselves would seem to be to ensure that they have proper access to work in normal employment conditions.

For women who are not gainfully employed, the traditional forms of social protection often offer the most effective guarantee of security. Maternity protection and the protection of derived rights can, as this study has shown, be developed still further. Efforts in this direction will be necessary as long as women are not fully integrated into the economic process: the development of personal rights with entitlements based on their own occupational activities will not be sufficient to protect them from marginalisation.

CONCLUSION

In tracing the action taken at international level to provide equal treatment for men and women and in studying the developments in national social security systems, we have been able both to define the scope of the equal treatment principle and to observe the many examples of discrimination against women which still exist, despite the progress already accomplished.

The extreme difficulty of judging whether men and women really are in "equal" situations makes it impossible to adopt the sole criterion of "equal social rights in equal situations". Instead, we may consider the problem in the following terms:

— social coverage identical to that provided for men, for women exercising an occupational activity, whatever the nature of the activity and the economic sector in which it is carried out;
— application of the same rules to both men and women in so far as they are in the same employment situation;
— adjustment of the rules when a category of workers experiences specific needs arising from a particular situation.

Compared with the situation in which economically active women found themselves some ten years ago, tangible progress has been made, as regards both the scope and the level of social protection. The protection of women who have withdrawn from the labour force, either temporarily or habitually, has also improved, particularly with the reinforcement of maternity protection and the development of derived rights. Extension of the notion of "workers with family responsibilities" is a corollary of women's increased participation in the economic process and of changing roles within the family.

Although on balance these are favourable developments, the fact that some progress has been accomplished should not be allowed to hide the fact that much remains to be done. Behind the many inequalities of treatment persisting in social security systems lie a multitude of economic and social distorsions—reflected in unequal training opportunities, lack of access to employment, undervaluation of the so-called female occupations—which create discriminatory situations for women. In other words, what is needed is a will to improve the overall position of women in society.

Periods of economic recession do not, unfortunately, lend themselves to the promotion of equal treatment for men and women—other concerns take priority. It is difficult to say how female employment will develop in the coming years: it has always been a regulating factor in the economic life of the industrialised countries and is closely dependent on the constraints imposed by general currents of expansion or recession. A lasting slowing down of economic growth could perpetuate situations which are discriminatory in respect of women, particularly since women constitute a large proportion of the unemployed.

Some of the developments which have taken place in the industrialised countries over the past few years are disturbing: the social protection acquired by workers in their own right does not provide an adequate response to such problems as unemployment, and the conditions to be satisfied for entitlement to such protection are ill-adapted to such forms of employment as casual labour or part-time work. In other words, the first and most important objective must be to ensure that women are fully integrated into the world of employment.

SELECTED BIBLIOGRAPHY

1. INTERNATIONAL LABOUR OFFICE, GENEVA

Conference reports

Women workers in a changing world (employment of women with family responsibilities), Report VI (1), International Labour Conference, 48th Session, 1964.

Equality of opportunity and treatment for women workers, Report VIII, International Labour Conference, 60th Session, 1975.

Employment (women with family responsibilities), General Survey by the Committee of Experts on the Application of Conventions and Recommendations, Report III (4B), International Labour Conference, 64th Session, 1978.

Equal opportunities and equal treatment for men and women workers: Workers with family responsibilities, Report VI (1), International Labour Conference, 66th Session, 1980.

Equal opportunities and equal treatment for men and women in employment, Report VII, International Labour Conference, 71st Session, 1985.

Employment promotion and social security, Report IV (1), International Labour Conference, 73rd Session, 1987.

Equality in employment and occupation, General Survey by the Committee of Experts on the Application of Conventions and Recommendations, Report III (4B), International Labour Conference, 75th Session, 1988.

Other publications

Social security in Africa: Trends, problems and prospects, by P. Mouton (1976).

Selected standards and policy statements of special interest to women workers adopted under the auspices of the International Labour Organisation (1980).

Introduction to social security (1984).

Into the twenty-first century: The development of social security, A report to the Director-General of the International Labour Office (1984).

Maternity benefits in the eighties, An ILO global survey (1964–84) (1985).

Working women in socialist countries: The fertility connection, edited by V. Bodrova and R. Anker (1985).

"Work and family; The child care challenge", *Conditions of Work Digest,* Vol. 7, 2/1988.

"Part-time work", *Conditions of Work Digest,* Vol. 8, 1/1989.

From pyramid to pillar: Population change and social security in Europe (1989).

Women in the world of work: Statistical analysis and projections to the year 2000, by S. Nuss with the collaboration of E. Denti and D. Viry. Women, Work and Development, 18.

2. INTERNATIONAL SOCIAL SECURITY ASSOCIATION (ISSA)

Conference reports

The relationship between family allowances and family incomes, reporter: B. Fragonard, Report VIII, XXIst General Assembly, Geneva, 3–13 October 1983.

Family benefits for special purposes, reporter: R. Arias-Perez, Report IX, XXIst General Assembly, Geneva, 3–13 October 1983.

Pension schemes for women and the importance of new structures of remunerated employment as they affect pension schemes for women, reporter: P. R. Fortier, Report II, XXIInd General Assembly, Montreal, 2–12 September 1986.

The evolution and financing of family benefits in the context of the economic crisis, reporter B. Fragonard, Report XI, XXIInd General Assembly, Montreal, 2-12 September 1986.

Family benefits provided for one-parent families, reporter: G. Mattyasovszky, Report X, XXIInd General Assembly, Montreal, 2–12 September 1986.

Studies and Research

Women and social security, No. 5 (Geneva, 1973).

The role of social services in social security: Trends and perspectives, No. 6 (Geneva, 1974).

Social security provisions in case of divorce, No. 11 (Geneva, 1978).

Social security and taxation, No. 13 (Geneva, 1979).

Equal treatment in social security, No. 27 (Geneva, 1988).

Social security documentation

American Series

Asignaciones familiares, No. 3 (Buenos Aires, 1982).

Asian Series

Changing family patterns and social security protection, No. 3 (New Delhi, 1979).

European Series

Social security and family policy, No. 8 (Geneva, 1983).

3. OECD, PARIS

Equal opportunities for women (1979).

Employment and unemployment of women in OECD countries, by L. Paukert (1984).

4. COUNCIL OF EUROPE, STRASBOURG

The concept of derived right and personal right in social security systems, having regard to the specific problems encountered in cases of derived right when the dependent relationship is broken off, preliminary study by Mr. Donis, Steering Committee for Social Security (October 1984).

Trends in social security legislation since 1974, Committee of Senior Officials responsible for the preparation of the 3rd Conference of European Ministers responsible for Social Security (March 1985).

Report of the Steering Committee for Social Security to the Committee of Ministers on the action taken by the Governments of Member States on Resolution 28 (1975) on social security for women at home (March 1985).

Rapport sur l'égalité entre femmes et hommes dans le domaine de la sécurité sociale, report by Mrs. Brunner, Steering Committee for Social Security (March 1985).

5. EUROPEAN ECONOMIC COMMUNITY

La mise en œuvre de l'égalité de traitement entre hommes et femmes en matière de sécurité sociale en ce qui concerne les prestations non soumises à la Directive 79/7/EEC du 19 décembre 1978: inventaire et propositions, Definitive synthesis report by Ms. C. Même, doc. V/1261/84-FR (Brussels, Commission of the European Communities, July 1984).

6. OTHER PUBLICATIONS

Aaron, B., and Farwell, D. F. (eds.). *The situation of women workers as regards labour legislation and social security legislation,* 10th International Congress of the International Society for Labour Law and Social Security, Washington, DC, 7–10 September 1982, Reports and Proceedings, Vol. III.

Bouillaguet-Bernard, P., Gawin-Ayel, A., and Outin, J. L. *Femmes au travail – prospérité et crise* (Paris, Economica, 1981).

Erié, S. P. *The conservative attack upon women and the welfare state in the United States: Potential for a new progressive alliance,* delivered at the Tocqueville Society Conference on Community Action and Public Policy (Paris, Institut d'études politiques, 1985).

Gazier, B. *La pauvreté unidimensionnelle* (Paris, Economica, 1981).

Janjič, M. *The recent developments in legislation regarding the employment of women in industrialised countries and its importance for industrial relations,* International Symposium on Women and Industrial Relations, International Institute for Labour Studies, Geneva, September 1978.

Kamerman, S. B. *Maternity and parental benefits and leaves,* Impact on Policy Series, Monograph No. 1 (New York, Columbia University, Autumn 1980).

Lawson R., and Townsend, P. *Responses to poverty: Lessons from Europe* (London, Heinemann, 1984).

Marsault, H. "Droits propres contre droits dérivés: l'individualisation des droits sociaux comme moyen d'améliorer la sécurité économique d'existence individuelle et familiale", in *Droit social* (Paris), Vol. 12, Dec. 1985, pp. 875–885.

Sabourin, A. *Le travail des femmes dans la CEE* (Paris, Economica, 1984).

Sullerot, E.: *Le statut matrimonial: ses conséquences juridiques, fiscales et sociales,* Report to the Economic and Social Council (Paris, 1984).

United States, Department of Health and Human Services, Social Security Administration. *Social security programs throughout the world, 1988,* Research Report No. 59 (Washington, DC, 1984).

7. REVIEW ARTICLES

International Labour Review, Geneva, ILO

Crijns L., and Laurent, A. "Action by the Commission of the European Communities in the field of social security", Sep.–Oct. 1978, pp. 569–581.

Euzéby, A. "Social security and part-time employment", 1985/5, pp. 545–557.

Gelber, S. M. "Social security and women: A partisan view", Dec. 1975, pp. 431–444.

Jiménez Butragueño, M. de los Angeles. "Protective legislation and equal opportunity and treatment for women in Spain", Mar.–Apr. 1982, pp. 185–198.

Landau, E. E. "Recent legislation and case law in the EEC on sex equality and employment", Jan.-Feb. 1984, pp. 53–70.

Laurent, A. "The elimination of sex discrimination in occupational social security systems in the EEC", Nov.–Dec. 1986, pp. 675–683.

Nakanishi, T. "Equality or protection? Protective legislation for women in Japan", Sep.–Oct. 1983, pp. 609–621.

Paoli, C. "Women workers and maternity: Some examples from Western Europe", Jan.–Feb. 1982, pp. 1–16.

Robinson, O. "Part-time employment in the European Community", May–June 1979, pp. 299–314.

Werneke, D. "The economic slowdown and women's employment opportunities", Jan–Feb. 1978, pp. 37–52.

International Social Security Review, Geneva, ISSA

Brocas, A.-M. "Equal treatment of men and women in social security: An overview", 1988, No. 3, pp. 231–249.

Drbohlav, V. "Protection and social security for working mothers in Czechoslovakia", 1984, No. 2, pp. 171–177.

Hyman, M. "Housewives' non-contributory invalidity pension: The case for abolition of the Household Duties Test in the United Kingdom", 1982, No. 3, pp. 319–332.

Kamerman, S. B., and Kahn, A. J. "Income transfers, work and the economic well-being of families with children: A comparative study", 1982, No. 3, pp. 345–382.

— "Single-parent, female-headed families in Western Europe: Social change and response", 1989, No. 1, pp. 3–34.

Laroque, P. "Social protection and the over-75s: What are the problems?", 1978, No. 3, pp. 267–284.

Messere, K. and Owens, J. "The treatment of dependent children under income tax and social welfare systems", 1979, No. 1, pp. 50–59.

Midgley, J. "Social assistance: An alternative form of social protection in developing countries", 1984, No. 3, pp. 247–264.

Münz, R., and Winterberger, H. "The Austrian welfare state: Social policy and income maintenance programs between 1970 and 1984", 1984, No. 3, pp. 300–314.

Paltiel, F. L. "Women and pensions in Canada", 1982, No. 3, pp. 333–344.

Poske, D. "Jurisprudence of the Federal Constitutional Court concerning the equality of men and women in the pensions insurance law of the Federal Republic of Germany", 1981, No. 2, pp. 175–183.

Skolnik, A. M. "Reform of occupational pensions in the United States of America", 1975, No. 3, pp. 229–241.

Solcher, H. "Sharing of pension rights in the event of divorce under German law", 1978, No. 3, pp. 308–317.

Villars, C. "Swiss sickness and maternity insurance", 1977, No. 2, pp. 170–188.

Weidner, J.: "Old-age security for farmers in the Federal Republic of Germany", 1984, No. 3, pp. 279–288.

"World Assembly on Aging", report, 1982, No. 4, pp. 584–590.

Droit Social, Paris

Baroin, D., and Loos, J. "Protection juridique et couverture sociale du travail à temps partiel en Europe", July–Aug. 1982.

Bichot, J. "Peut-on en finir avec les droits dérivés? Le cas de l'assurance maladie", Jan. 1985.

Cuvillier, R. "L'épouse au foyer: une charge injustifiée pour la collectivité", Dec. 1977.

Gandouin, F. "Pour une approche socio-économique du travail temporaire", July–Aug. 1982.

Ruellan, R. "La femme et la sécurité sociale", Jan. 1976.

Teyssié, B.: "Le travail à temps partiel (ordonnance No. 82–271 du 26 mars 1982)", May 1982.

Liaisons sociales, Paris

Travail précaire et à temps partiel, Special issue 8831, Sep. 1982.

Revue Belge de sécurité sociale, Brussels, Ministry of Social Welfare

"Des chances égales pour les femmes", under the heading Mouvement des idées et des faits, Sep.–Oct. 1984.

Japan Labor Bulletin, Tokyo, Japan Institute of Labor

"Actual conditions and legal problems relating to part-time employment", Jan. 1984.

Industrial Law Journal, London, Industrial Law Society

Ellis, E., and Morrell, P. "Sex discrimination in pension schemes: Has Community law changed the rules?", Mar. 1982.

Social and Labour Bulletin, Geneva, ILO

1975–85

Legislative Series, Geneva, ILO

1975–85

Women at Work, Geneva, ILO

1975–85

Women of Europe, Brussels, Commission of the European Communities

1981–85

Social Europe, Brussels, Commission of the European Communities